LENIN'S CHILDHOOD

This title is one of a series published to commemorate the centenary of V. I. Lenin's death. The others are as follows:

Imperialism and the National Question, V. I. Lenin
The State and Revolution, V. I. Lenin

The Lenin Scenario, Tariq Ali
Not by Politics Alone: The Other Lenin, edited by Tamara Deutscher

LENIN'S CHILDHOOD

ISAAC DEUTSCHER

Original Introduction by Tamara Deutscher

*Introduction to the Anniversary
Edition by Gonzalo Pozo*

VERSO

London • New York

This edition first published by Verso 2024
First published by Oxford University Press 1970
© Verso Books 2024
Introduction to the anniversary edition © Gonzalo Pozo 2024

1 3 5 7 9 10 8 6 4 2

Verso
UK: 6 Meard Street, London W1F 0EG
US: 388 Atlantic Avenue, Brooklyn, NY 11217
versobooks.com

Verso is the imprint of New Left Books

ISBN-13: 978-1-80429-277-8
ISBN-13: 978-1-80429-279-2 (US EBK)
ISBN-13: 978-1-80429-278-5 (UK EBK)

British Library Cataloguing in Publication Data
A catalogue record for this book is available from the British Library

Library of Congress Cataloging-in-Publication Data
Names: Deutscher, Isaac, 1907–1967, author.
Title: Lenin's childhood / Isaac Deutscher.
Description: Anniversary edition. | London ; New York : Verso, 2024. |
  "First published by Oxford University Press 1970." | Includes
  bibliographical references.
Identifiers: LCCN 2023037198 (print) | LCCN 2023037199 (ebook) | ISBN
  9781804292778 (paperback) | ISBN 9781804292792 (ebk)
Subjects: LCSH: Lenin, Vladimir Il'ich, 1870–1924—Childhood and youth. |
  Lenin, Vladimir Il'ich, 1870–1924—Family. | Ul'ianov family. |
  Ul'ianovsk (Russia)—Biography. | Heads of state—Soviet
  Union—Biography.
Classification: LCC DK254.L44 D48 2024 (print) | LCC DK254.L44 (ebook) |
  DDC 947.084/1092 [B]—dc23/eng/20230822
LC record available at https://lccn.loc.gov/2023037198
LC ebook record available at https://lccn.loc.gov/2023037199

Printed and bound by CPI Group (UK) Ltd, Croydon, CR0 4YY

CONTENTS

INTRODUCTION TO THE ANNIVERSARY EDITION: THE UNFINISHED BIOGRAPHY OF THE UNFINISHED REVOLUTION

Isaac Deutscher lived and worked passionately across the geographical and linguistic boundaries as well as the political ruptures which divided and assembled twentieth-century Europe. His achievements as a writer, activist and historian can be seen as an attempt to interrogate and bridge the century's many breaks and hopes. The author of the (posthumously published) *Non-Jewish Jew*—strangely and yet predictably, the work he is best known for today—was deeply aware of the dialectical relation between fracture and continuity, even when reflecting on his own life.

A brief autobiographical sketch, dated December 1965, begins, 'I was born (3 April, 1907) near Cracow, the Polish medieval capital, into an orthodox Jewish family in which some of the traditions of medieval Judaism lived on.'[1] The sparse and yet synthetic self-portrait is a narrative (rehearsed in four earlier versions written in 1948–9, 1955–6, 1957,

---

1 Isaac Deutscher, 'Biographical Data', December 1965, *Isaac Deutscher Papers* 167, International Institute of Social History, Amsterdam. Henceforth, all references to documents in the Deutscher Amsterdam archive are listed as *IDP*.

vii

1962) threaded by the laconic enumeration, not simply of his considerable intellectual accomplishments, but of transitions, anticipations and, perhaps most of all, transgressions.[1] 'The first act of my self-determination was to renounce religious orthodoxy, to write poetry in Polish.' Deutscher's earliest 'heretical' stance—the decision to become a Polish poet and translator of lyrical works from Yiddish, Hebrew, German and Latin—came hand in hand with a confrontation with his family, and with the refusal to follow 'an ecclesiastical' path, rebelling against his father's wishes. 'The next act of my self-determination was to renounce my bourgeois environment and become a member of the outlawed Communist Party of Poland' (KPP). Barely eighteen, Deutscher left his family in Cracow and moved, penniless, to Warsaw. There he continued publishing reviews and articles in the national press and threw himself into activism, serving as editor on several party organs, as well as penning 'political commentaries, illegal manifestoes and leaflets, addressing workers, organizing even peasants, conducting, as a soldier, underground propaganda in Piłsudski's army, and all the time dodging the Gendarmerie and the political police'. Of course, Deutscher's radicalization was part of a deeper intellectual conversion. He would abandon poetry for criticism, moving on to philosophy, history and eventually economics—'all very poetic subjects', he added, in an earlier memo written in 1950.[2] This (only partly) tongue-in-cheek remark reappeared fully fledged in the 1965 version: 'the successive steps of my renunciation of the bourgeois *Weltanschauung*, and of my study and acceptance of Marxism and Leninism . . . opened my eyes to the pure poetry of the class struggle and socialist revolution.' As it happens, Vladimir Ilyich Ulyanov, the subject of *Lenin's Childhood*, had expressed a similar sentiment, if barbed by

1 Deutscher, untitled autobiographical note, 1957; 'Biographical Notes', 1948–49, *IDP* 167; 'Biographical Notes', 1955–56. These items are in *IDP* 167; also 'Biographical Data', 1962, *IDP 202*.
2 Deutscher, untitled, 1957, *IDP* 167.

considerably more ironic distance: 'I am still "in love" [*ya vsyo eshchyo "vliublyon"*] with Marx and Engels,' he wrote to his lover, Inessa Armand, in a letter from 30 January 1917, 'and I cannot take any abuse to them tranquilly. No, these were the real people. It is necessary to learn from them—we must not leave that basis.'[1]

It would be in Soviet Russia and Ukraine, where he had been sent by the party in 1931, that Deutscher was able to examine the realities of life under the first Five-Year Plan first-hand. The experience was formative, only this time, not lyrical. Impressed and yet alarmed by what he saw, his travels in the Soviet Union roused in him a new heretical impulse. On his return to Warsaw, Deutscher began ('with three or four other comrades') to organize the first anti-Stalinist opposition against, yet still inside, the KPP. The group accused the party and the Comintern of neglecting the threat of fascism and Nazism, and demanded joint action with the socialists against Hitler in Germany and Piłsudski in Poland. They also blasted 'Stalin and his henchmen for leading European communism to catastrophe and denying us freedom of expression'.[2] During the summer of 1932, still acting as editor of the Yiddish-language *Literarishe Tribune* (a legal cultural KPP monthly), Deutscher distilled the opposition's critique in an impassioned and foretelling text entitled 'The Danger of Culture-Barbarism in Germany', under the pseudonym A. Krakovski, meaning one from Cracow.[3] (A fellow oppositionist, Joshke Rabinovitsh, had discreetly inserted Deutscher's essay among the typeset materials for the July issue just before it went to press.) This and ensuing events have come be known in KPP history as the 'Krakovski affair': after publishing his

1 V. I. Lenin, '360. [Letter to] I. F. Armand', in *Polnoe sobranie sochinenii*, vol. 49, Izdatel'stvo Politicheskoi Literatury, Moscow, 1970, p. 379, my translation; cf. V. I. Lenin, *Collected Works*, vol. 35, Progress Publishers, Moscow, 1973, p. 281; and Lars T. Lih, *Lenin*, Critical Lives, London, Reaktion Books, 2011, p. 13.

2 Deutscher 1965, *IDP* 167.

3 A. Krakovski [Isaac Deutscher], 'Di gefar fun kultur-barbarizm in Daytshland', *Literarishe Tribune*, 1932, no. 7, pp. 1–4.

denunciation of the party, Deutscher was immediately dismissed from his editorial tasks and a riposte was quickly published on the following issue of *Literarishe Tribune* pronouncing his piece 'totally false, harmful and anti-proletarian'.[1] Invited to recant (in vain) later that autumn, Deutscher was officially expelled from the party during the KKP's 6th Congress in November. From that point on, Deutscher continued his struggle more or less on his own, though in the orbit of various anti-Stalinist platforms—once more in it but not completely of it. 'Like my comrades,' he wrote, 'I was persecuted simultaneously by the Piłsudskist police and the Stalinists; but as Poland had an anti-communist government then, no decent person in the West protested in the name of "cultural freedom."'[2]

In April 1939, he made a new break, moving to London as foreign correspondent for the Warsaw Polish-language Zionist daily *Nasz Przegląd* (Our Review). When World War II broke out in September, he enrolled with the Polish Army in Exile, but ended up spending most that time in a 'punitive' camp in Scotland, for denouncing the rampant anti-Semitism in its ranks.[3] After his release in 1942, Deutscher returned to London and began a successful career as correspondent for the *Economist* and *Observer*, but transitioned once more in 1946: 'jaded with journalism and unwilling to wage the

1 Moyshe Levin, 'Tsu der frage fun "kultur barbarizm" in Daytshland (oyfn rand fun kh. Krakovskis artikl in forikn num. "Lit. Tribune")', *Literarishe Tribune*, 1932, no. 8, pp. 3–8, p. 3. Levin remarked on the fact that Deutscher had been venting his own views exclusively, acting behind the back of the other editors. See also, Joanna Nalewajko Kulikov, 'Yiddish Form, Communist Content: Jewish Communist Writers in Warsaw in the 1930s', *Polin*, no. 28, 2016, pp. 351–70, especially, pp. 353–4, and also Jack Jacobs, 'Communist Questions, Jewish Answers: Polish Jewish dissident communists of the inter-war era', *Polin*, no. 5, 2005, pp. 369–79. Deutscher's own appraisal of the KKP's trajectory does not delve into the anti-Stalinist opposition: see Deutscher [1958] 'The Tragedy of the Polish Communist Party' in Perry Anderson (ed.), *Marxism, Wars and Revolutions,* London: Verso, 1984, pp. 91–127.

2 Deutscher 1965, *IDP* 167.

3 Deutscher, 'Attempt to write his memoirs', *IDP* 203; see also, Gonzalo Pozo, '"I must start Completely Alone." On Isaac Deutscher's Wartime Years in London', *London Review of Books,* vol. 45, no 3, 2023.

Cold War, I withdrew from Fleet St.'[1] After that, Deutscher remained an independent voice, frequently contributing articles on Soviet and international affairs and devoting himself to historical work. His story thenceforth is much better known and need not be rehearsed here, except to say that it was, above all, his *Stalin* (1949) and especially his monumental Trotsky trilogy—*The Prophet Armed* (1954), *The Prophet Unarmed* (1959) and *The Prophet Outcast* (1963)—that earned him international fame.[2]

Deutscher embarked on the ceaseless labour behind these books from outside academia, sustaining himself and his family as a freelancer, but, despite these and other difficulties, *Stalin* and, especially, *Trotsky* (two very different kinds of biography) are now unquestionably Marxist classics. At the time of their release, they roused political acclaim and controversy, more or less in equal measure, both from the left and from the right. What virtually everyone converged on was an intense admiration for his rigour and high scholarly standards, and in particular for his mastery of English prose. Several have compared him to Joseph Conrad.[3] Deutscher himself, not always the most modest of intellectuals and now buried under the stacks of unpublished words in the archive, can still be heard almost excessively protesting a clearly anticipated compliment: 'I was careful not to emulate my famous countryman [Conrad] in bringing the Polish literary idiom into the English language. I have tried instead to learn a little English from Gibbon and Macauley.'[4]

Stalin and *Trotsky* are, of course, part of a broader project, which would have been crowned by the appearance of *Lenin*,

1 Deutscher 1965, *IDP* 167.

2 Deutscher, *Stalin: A Political Biography,* London, Oxford University Press, [1949] 1961; the Trotsky trilogy was reissued by Verso in January 2004.

3 Two more recent examples are Perry Anderson, 'The Legacy of Isaac Deutscher', in *A Zone of Engagement*, London, Verso, 1992, pp. 56–76, p. 56; and Neil Davidson, 'Isaac Deutscher: The Prophet, His Biographer and the Watchtower', *International Socialism*, vol. 2, no. 104, 2004.

4 Deutscher 1965, *IDP* 167.

but not only by *Lenin*. It has been often said that, together, the three biographies would have represented the fulfilment of Deutscher's lifework, constituting 'a triptych of some artistic unity'. Deutscher wrote as much in his 1965 memo. Tamara Deutscher repeated the assertion in the original introduction to the 1970 edition of *Lenin's Childhood*, and still others have echoed it.[1] What is less often noted, however, is that, in its turn, the 'triptych' was not just meant to explore the role of key individuals in the broader politics, successes and disappointments of the Bolshevik Revolution, but was also intended to hang on a previous, exhaustive study of the economic, social and cultural history of the Soviet Union. This broader frame—a non-biographical exploration of the history of the USSR—was an endeavour which Deutscher had envisaged even before his exile from Poland in 1939 and which he was still promising in his autobiographical notes from the late 1940s, while he frantically freelanced for the British press and rushed to finish *Stalin*.[2] However, the 'Social History of the USSR', as he refers to it in his notes, and for which he was offered a $300 advance in 1952, would never appear fully realized and complete. Like its object, it remained a moving target, a thing in permanent development. Its basic arguments and projections have to be reassembled from other works over the decades, from *Soviet Trade Unions* (1950), through innumerable essays and articles over the years, *Russia after Stalin* (1953), *The Great Contest* (1960), all the way to the last book published during his lifetime—a kind of synthesis and testament, based on his 1966–67 Trevelyan Lectures—*The Unfinished Revolution*.

For all its merits and breadth, the result (Deutscher's complete map of the Soviet Union's achievements and

---

1 Ibid.; Tamara Deutscher's introduction in this volume, p. 1; David Caute, *Isaac and Isaiah: The Covert Punishment of a Cold War Heretic*, London, Yale University Press, 2013, p. 13.

2 Pozo, 'I Must Start Completely Alone'; Deutscher 1965, *IDP* 167; 'Biographical Notes', 1948–49, *IDP* 167.

prospects) is also, in a sense, unfinished, and he was unwilling and unable to work according to any thematic order in the execution of the grand plan. On leaving his career as a full-time journalist in 1946, he was keen to take on all aspects of the USSR—history, economics, culture, politics, and biography—simultaneously. But the groundwork for *Lenin* was there from the start, including a statement of agreement with Oxford University Press signed as early as 1950 for a (provisionally entitled) *Life of Lenin*, coinciding with the research which resulted in the first two instalments of his *Trotsky*. As finishing the *Prophet* trilogy ended up taking most of his time and energy until 1963, Deutscher postponed writing *Lenin* until 1964, when he and Tamara began collecting old quotes and fragments, and drawing up new chronologies and preparatory notes.[1] In the Spring of 1965, an (updated) contract with Oxford was agreed for a projected two-volume Lenin biography, and, this time, with the publisher offering a handsome advance payable over the following four years.[2] Alas, Deutscher would be able to manage only a fairly complete draft of the first *Lenin* chapter during the entire period between his decision to abandon full-time journalism to become a historian, in 1946, and his sudden death in summer 1967.

The final version of that chapter, re-edited and published posthumously by Tamara with the Oxford University Press, is the present book. Inevitably limited in scope, it focusses on the origins of the Ulyanov family and takes the reader from Lenin's early years to the execution of his brother, Alexander. Unsurprisingly then, *Lenin's Childhood* reveals only a sliver of the research Deutscher had undertaken for this biography, as even Tamara acknowledged in her 1970

1 Deutscher, 'Notes, Drafts, Final Version and Page Proofs for Lenin's Childhood', *IDP* 151, four folders, especially *IDP* 151a.

2 'John Brett (OUP) to Isaac Deutscher', 20 May 1965, *IDP* 216. The advance mentioned is the very generous sum of $50,000 (around half a million dollars in today's money), payable over four years. That an academic publisher could and, most of all, would offer such terms is surely food for thought.

pitch to the publisher: 'I assume that factual material about Lenin's childhood has been used by other biographers. But the strength of Isaac's chapter lies precisely in the originality or viewpoint and in the presentation.'[1] Whatever documentary novelty and historical perspective Deutscher might have been able to bring to a finished *Lenin* can only be provisionally formulated from the preparatory notes left in the archive.

Partly for the purposes of promoting *Stalin*, and partly to begin work on *Trotsky*, the Deutschers began preparations to travel to McCarthyite America, with support of a Rockefeller Foundation grant obtained in 1950. Getting travel visas turned out to be a fraught process; Deutscher refused to recant, as required, from his Marxist convictions or from his communist past. When an offer of a permit came in exchange for stating he had abandoned his politics for a return to the 'rabbinical tradition', Deutscher refused again, submitting, according to Tamara's rendition, a declaration declining to plead his involvement in the KPP, and arguing instead that 'the experience of my association with the Communist Party was on the whole a valuable one for my own mental development and further work'. Always, according to Tamara, he added, 'One reason for my strong opposition to the CP has been my disgust with the recantations practiced in its ranks. This disgust has remained very strong with me; and it applies to all sorts of recantations by whomever and for whatever reasons they may be required.'[2] After some months of litigation, the visas were finally granted, and, before the year was out, Isaac and Tamara Deutscher began their extensive research in Stanford and especially in the Trotsky archives deposited in Harvard's Houghton Library—all in preparation for *The Prophet Armed* and *The Prophet Unarmed*. '[T]he notebooks from the Houghton Library', recalled Tamara, 'bear here and there the marks

1 Tamara Deutscher, 'Letter to John Bell (OUP)', 21 January 1970, *IDP* 310.
2 Tamara Deutscher, 'Work in Progress', in David Horowitz (ed.), *Isaac Deutscher: The Man and His Work*, London, Macdonald, 1971, pp. 57–93, 67; cf. Caute, *Isaac and Isaiah*, p. 28.

of a big L in red pencil; material which had been collected for the Stalin biography bears sometimes a remark: To be consulted for *Lenin.*' There was more than this, in fact.

The Trotsky notebooks contain passages marked out with a red L, indeed; the time served by Deutscher at US libraries, however, produced two densely packed pads, written in English, Polish and Russian, one marked 'Hoover Notebook', and another labelled 'For Lenin—Stanford'.[1] The 'Hoover' notes are almost entirely devoted to the preparation of *Trotsky*, with lists and excerpts from different letters and articles by him in *Iskra* and *Pravda,* as well as annotations from the correspondence between Martov and Axelrod. These notes also include a brief fragment from Trotsky's *Vie de Lénine*, related in particular to his childhood and youth. The 'Stanford' notes, by contrast, consist of various excerpts from articles in early Russian revolutionary newspapers, especially *Pravda*, *Iskra, Nashe Slovo*, *Nachalo* and *Golos*, along with, among other sources, fragments from Lunacharsky's *Revolutionary Silhouettes* and Martov's *History of the Russian Social Democracy.* The bulk of these annotations deal with the evolution of the Bolshevik Party into the first years of the revolution, with most of the original references dated between 1905 and 1920, and most segments relevant to Lenin's personality and role are highlighted in red without comments. In both sets, especially in the "Stanford" notes, the overall concern seems to be that of elucidating the political differences and points of convergence in the relation between Lenin and Trotsky.

Deutscher would be back to the US in 1959, thanks to an invitation from the Dafoe Foundation and the Canadian Institute of International Affairs. This gave him a chance to return to Harvard and complete his work in the Houghton Library, specifically in the closed section of the Trotsky archives. According to Trotsky's will, these holdings (mostly

1 Isaac and Tamara Deutscher, 'Stanford and Hoover Notebooks', 1950, *IDP* 239.

private correspondence) should have remained closed until 1980, but Deutscher obtained early access thanks to the intercession of Natalia Sedova. The result is *The Prophet Outcast,* which was finally published in 1963, after fifteen years of work. Deutscher would only return to the US again in Spring 1965, not, this time, on an academic invitation, but on an offer to partake at the national Vietnam teach-in, Washington. The event would be followed by thousands, either on site in the Sheraton Hotel or on television, and brought in figures such as Arthur Schlesinger and Zbigniew Brzezinski, arguing in favour of US policy, or Hans Morgenthau, arguing against it. In his previous visits, Deutscher had been forced to be circumspect, avoiding public speeches and engagements of this kind, and keeping to academic exchanges and research. Now, having resumed work on *Lenin*, Deutscher and the politics of the sixties had begun to positively charge one another. He was back to the US for a new Berkeley teach-in come 1966, and again between March and May 1967, combining a visiting fellowship at Harpur College (State University of New York, Binghamton) with more teach-ins and demonstrations, as well as with work with the Russell Tribunal into war crimes in Vietnam in Stockholm and Copenhagen later that spring. The messages home from Deutscher in those weeks relate a mix of excitement and misgivings about a new radicalism in the US. After participating in a large anti-Vietnam demonstration in New York on 15 April 1967, for instance, Deutscher writes to Tamara: '[L]et me only add that this was an event just as impressive for its size and élan as for its political immaturity, to put it mildly', and yet, 'this movement will leave deeper traces and have more continuity than the CND in England . . . the number of people inclined to a serious study of Marxism is really quite considerable'. Worried about his high level of activity and his deteriorating health, Tamara was, perhaps, the more prophetic: 'I really think it was a mistake to accept the invitation to Binghamton etc. It would have been much better if he could concentrate on *Lenin*.'[1] Too late: Deutscher would suffer a fatal heart attack in Rome later that August.

During those last two years, Deutscher and Tamara had been concentrating on the preparatory sources for the first drafts of *Lenin's Childhood*, as well as materials and some ideas for a further section on his youth after 1887 and on the question of his political radicalization. Beyond rougher drafts of the *Childhood*, however, Deutscher left only a fragment of an earlier version of the same text, written in 1966, but eventually discarded.[2] His notes on the early Lenin from the mid-1960s draw on over fifteen years of research, as attested by the links drawn between them and the Stanford Notebook, as well as by the constant tussle between English and Polish, often within the same paragraphs. It is noteworthy, that, by the time Deutscher had turned to *Lenin's Childhood*, a number of well-known English biographies were widely available.[3] By and large, he seems to have disregarded them, feeling clearly confident in the lines of investigation and sources which he had already opened in the 1950s, and which he then set to develop, relying mostly on Soviet historiographical material. He was more interested in following the news about archival releases and studies in Russia (particularly, in *Voprosy Istorii KPSS*) than in following Lenin scholarship in Britain or the US. Also, in continuity with his early research, Deutscher reconstructed *Lenin's Childhood* above all from two sources. The first of these is Trotsky's magnificent *Vie de Lénine*, whose insights and descriptions he both praised and occasionally queried— 'Where does he get this?' he writes, on a particularly

1 Deutscher, 'Letter to Tamara', 16 April 1967, *IDP* 90; Tamara Deutscher, 'Letter to Amelie Rorty', 27 April 1967, *IDP* 67.

2 Deutscher, *IDP* 151a.

3 David Shub's *Lenin* had appeared in 1948, and in the year when Deutscher turned to *Lenin*, no fewer than three new biographies were published in English: Angelica Balabanoff, *Impressions on Lenin*, Ann Arbor, University of Michigan Press, 1964; Robert Payne, *The Life and Death of Lenin*, New York, Simon and Schuster, 1964; and Louis Fischer, *The Life of Lenin*, New York, Harper and Row, 1964.

xvii

evocative recreation by Trotsky of the effects of Alexander's execution on the rest of the Ulyanov family. Around half of the preparatory notes for *Lenin's Childhood* are based on an admiring yet critical dialogue with Trotsky's own appraisal, questioning some and confirming most of it as he doubled-checked each detail. The rest of the groundwork is heavily based on the short volume *The Childhood and School Years of Ilich*, a memoir written by Anna Ilyichna Ulyanova-Elizarova, Lenin's older sister.[1] Elizarova had produced this text on commission from the Moscow Institute of Lenin (later the Institute for Marxism–Leninism) shortly after her brother's death in 1924. In the course of her research, Elizarova discovered that their grandfather, Aleksander Dmitrievich Blank, had been (unbeknownst to Lenin or herself) a Jewish convert from Ukraine, originally named Srul (or Yisroel) Moishevich.[2] Elizarova was told to suppress this information from her memoir, and despite her written objections to Stalin in both 1932 and 1934, Lenin's Jewish lineage was kept out of her book—and thus out of Deutscher's. In his notes, he still raises the question: 'Trotsky has no doubt about the Mongol admixture in Lenin and the German one. Blank's wife is a German. Of this there is no doubt. But who is Blank himself?' The answer would remain a Soviet state secret until the Glasnost period and now lends an unexpected depth to Deutscher's opening statement that 'the origins of the Ulyanov family are uncertain'—as uncertain as they had been contested.[3]

1 All references to the sources used by Deutscher for *Lenin's Childhood* are to *IDP* 151a; A. I. Ulyanova, *Detskie i szkol'nie gody Il'icha,* Gosudarstvennoe izdatel'stvo detskoi literatury, Moscow, Ministerstva Prosveshcheniya RSFSR, 1955. Deutscher does not seem to have known the similar and more or less contemporary collection of vignettes from Lenin's youth compiled and published by the Marx-Engels-Lenin Institute and published shortly after Elizarova's memoir: *Lenin v Samare 1889–93. Sbornik Vospominanii* [Lenin in Samara: Collected Memories], Moscow, Partiinoe Izdatel'stvo, 1933.

2 Dmitri Volkogonov, *Lenin: A New Biography,* London, New Press, 1994, p. 5; see also, Yohanan Petrovski-Shtern, *Lenin's Jewish Question*, New Haven, Yale University Press, 2010.

3 Deustcher, this volume, p. 1.

Always relying on Trotsky and Elizarova, Deutscher also draws the elements in *Lenin's Childhood* from several other points of reference. The first of these is Ivan Goncharov's novel *Oblomov*, a Russian classic set in Lenin's hometown, Simbirsk, whose eponymous protagonist would become a symbol of torpor, ennui and provincial backwardness. Deutscher takes down Goncharov's remark that the place was 'not a city but a graveyard', elsewhere citing Trotsky's comment that 'whoever wanted to learn to detest feudal barbarism should have been born [there]'. With some excitement, Deutscher remarks in his notes that Goncharov still lived there at the time of Lenin's birth and deploys a similarly sleepy and slow mood in the pages which make up his 'description of Simbirsk'—the motif is also present in Trotsky's *Vie de Lenine*. The importance of Goncharov goes beyond travelogue: the social, political, and economic horizons of Simbirsk were just as stifling as its spiritual atmosphere, heavily weighing on (and radically limiting) the prospects of social advancement for the up-and-coming liberal intelligentsia to which Lenin's family belonged. Trotsky and Elizarova, as well as Deutscher, eventually link this notion to the death of Lenin's father.

In planning the earliest stages of this book, Deutscher tried to understand the extent to which Lenin had been influenced by his brother's populist convictions and, especially, the ideas of Nikolai Chernyshevsky, a radical thinker and writer, author of the novel *What Is to Be Done?* [*Chto delat?*] and one of the intellectual engines behind the Russian Narodniks of the 1860s and 1870s. In particular, Deutscher's materials take up the role of his work on Lenin's politicization after his brother's execution. They include copied-out excerpts from a text by Plekhanov on Chernyshevsky's novel: '[W]e all drew from him both moral strength and the faith for the future.' In the event, this material never made it into *Lenin's Childhood*. Lenin would only imbibe Chernyshevsky's work beginning in 1888, and, as we have seen, Deutscher's book never got that far into his subject's life. Still, the presence of this source among Deutscher's papers tells us that subsequent chapters would have polemicized with Trotsky's conviction that Lenin, though increasingly a Marxist, was still clinging to the Narodnik tradition at least into 1891. 'This is not quite convincing,' writes Deutscher in his notes, 'because it is based on the assumption that the young Lenin had not yet read Plekhanov, or if he read him, could not understand him.' Splitting hairs, perhaps, since Deutscher and Trotsky do agree on the fundamental point: 'Trotsky unexpectedly and very wittily points out that, after Sasha's execution, what Vladimir did was precisely to follow in his footsteps, and not, as others say, to look for a more efficacious way.'[1] In any case, foregrounding Alexander Ulyanov's (Sasha's) short life and politics was key in Deutscher's chapter for other reasons. His preparatory notes include several copied fragments from Sasha's family correspondence published in *Vaprosy Istorii* in 1966, including a letter addressed to his mother and sister, asking them to forgive him for their suffering, sent just three days after his death sentence. For Deutscher, Alexander's importance in Lenin's development was not politics alone. Ultimately, Sasha is the character against (and on) which young Volodya struggles to sculpt his own personality. Deutscher's notes are quite explicit about this: 'the tension between Sasha and Vladimir [is] like the typical relation between two brothers in Adler—the contrast of temperaments'. This psycho-political chord sounds fortissimo during the final pages of *Lenin's Childhood*, as the noose tightens around Alexander's life and the Ulyanov family. It is here that the real structure of the chapter is revealed, and that we see young Lenin sharing the stage with Deutscher's other, ghostly protagonist. As Deutscher writes in the closing paragraph,

1 This is a reference to Soviet lore. 'During Soviet times, a workman trying to find a better solution to some difficulty might say optimistically, "We'll go another way, Sasha." The Sasha of this semi-proverb is Alexander Ulyanov': in Lih, *Lenin*, p. 23.

The name of Alexander does not occur in any of Lenin's books, articles, speeches, or even in his letters to his mother and sisters. In all the fifty-five volumes of the latest and most complete Russian edition of his Works, Alexander is mentioned almost incidentally and only twice . . . So extraordinary a reticence could not have been ascribed to frigidity of feeling: on the contrary, it covered an emotion too deep to be uttered and too painful ever to be recollected in tranquillity.[1]

This passage and the full force of Deutscher's last pages (quite literally, his last pages as historian) are deeply moving: but they are also dangerous. The search for the key which opens up the mind of a biography's subject can generate, of course, a 'mirror in mirror' situation. If Lenin's 'reticence' to speak about Sasha was born out of trauma, what might one say about Deutscher's own tragedy—the death of his mother, father, sister and brother in (or on the way to) the Nazi extermination camps between 1942–43—a trauma which he himself mentioned, almost incidentally and only once or twice, and which unfolded just as he was starting a brilliant career as a journalist?

It is perfectly conceivable that the elements which mark *Lenin's Childhood* would have also marked Deutscher's *Lenin*, had he lived to complete the work. It would have been a welcome and expert reinterpretation of his subject's life and legacy and, to say the least, made for an unforgettable read, though perhaps not necessarily one able to boast the same degree of historiographical relevance and novelty as his *Trotsky* trilogy. Nothing like Deutscher's access to Trotsky's closed archive in the 1950s would have been available to him while working on *Lenin*: the best he might have hoped for in terms of uncovering novel sources had already happened after Khrushchev's Twentieth Congress speech

1 Deutscher, *Lenin's Childhood*, p. 67.

and de-Stalinization. Further, while *Stalin* and *Lenin* throw up huge questions and historical dilemmas, these were ones which did not represent a special challenge for Deutscher: he had been reckoning with them politically for most of his adult life. Indeed, by the mid-1960s (and even before), Deutscher was not alone in intellectually seeking to save Lenin from Stalinism.[1] It is probably fair to say that finding his ground with Trotsky and *his* legacy would have remained the bigger challenge for him. Humanizing Lenin and his politics, on the other hand—tearing him down from his Soviet pedestal (while pulling him up from the flames of hell to which the Cold War had condemned him in the West)— was something he had been doing all along. Finally, in the context of Deutscher's broader oeuvre, *Lenin* would have certainly, perhaps primarily, confirmed two of his central convictions. Firstly, it would have cemented Deutscher's belief that the Bolshevik Revolution had been changing under its own temporality and not merely collapsed under some iron law of revolution; that it was a work unfinished, plagued with disaster, horrors, and mistakes, but also still alive with potential and promise. As he reasoned during an interview on a German radio during the late 1950s, 'I think there is, in every revolution, much that is irrational, and much that is much more rational [*vieles, viel mehr rationelles*].' Between political disenchantment and withdrawal, or mindless dogmatic adherence to 'really existing' socialism then, Deutscher saw his role as that of presenting the USSR as it actually was, or at least, as he actually saw it, upholding its more rational aspects while rejecting and denouncing the irrational ones. As he continued in that interview, the point was 'to break with Stalinism in the name of Marxism'.[2]

1 Among others, two works with an interpretation often overlapping with Deutscher's had appeared, or were about to, at the time of his death: Moshe Lewin, *Lenin's Last Struggle*, New York, Random House, 1968; and Marcel Liebman, *Le léninisme sous Lénine*, two volumes, Paris, Seuil, 1973; cf. with Isaac Deutscher, 'Lenin's Last Dilemma', *American Socialist*, vol. 5, no. 7, April 1959.

2 Deutscher, Stuttgart radio interview, unlabeled (1958?), GB1247 (old

Secondly, *Lenin* would have also confirmed Deutscher's deep conviction that alternatives had been possible, and that one day, these might indeed reopen.

Projecting Deutscher's *Lenin* from the posthumous *Lenin's Childhood* in this way is to a certain extent inevitable. Unsurprisingly, most of the (generally positive if relatively scant) reviews, either in the general press or in academic journals, focused on the book's unfulfilled potential, on the question of the alternative temporalities of the Russian Revolution and on the tall order of understanding it dispassionately within a firmly Marxist perspective. As the historian Louis Menashe noted in the pages of the *Nation*, for instance, '[I]t seems clear—and Deutscher recognized this in the last years before his death—that Stalin had ruptured revolutionary continuity in so profound a way as to defeat the possibility of a democratic socialism in the USSR for a long time to come.' He went on: 'writing at the height of the cold war, Deutscher had detached the socialist ideal from the falsified Stalinist definition of it'.[1] In a similar vein, though in a very different style, Christopher Hitchens also reviewed the book for the *New Statesman*, raising some of the same concerns: 'Deutscher was certain to give us further insights into two large questions which recur in his other essays: the extent to which the Soviet Union is a class society, and the capacity of the bureaucracy to reform itself.' He added, '*Lenin* would have been ideal for such a discussion.'[2]

With the benefit of much historical hindsight, *Lenin* might not have been so ideal, because whatever Deutscher's expectations of democratic reform, the underlying questions he had been asking captured much of what was tragic in the

---

indexing system), *IDP* 337, my translation; the question focuses on the theme of 'heretics and renegades', see Deutscher, *Heretics and Renegades: And Other Essays*, Maddison, WI, Bobbs Merrill, [1955] 1969.

1 Louis Menashe, 'What Did Lenin Mean? Review of Isaac Deutscher's *Lenin's Childhood*', *Nation*, 15 March 1971, pp. 341–4; see also *IDP* 189.

2 Christopher Hitchens, 'Review of Isaac Deutscher's *Lenin's Childhood*', *New Statesman*, 11 December 1970; *IDP* 189.

revolutionary movements in the twentieth century. His optimistic conviction that Russia might yet change was, at the same time, an admission that it had indeed changed, in some ways beyond recognition, and in the process, much of the original 1917 had been lost or sacrificed. The more painful aspects of that recognition, the collective and intimate debate between hoping and disarming (ultimately always resolved by affirming hope) came through quite clearly, particularly when Deutscher stepped out of his public persona. In the spring of 1956, for instance, Deutscher scribbled down a five-page imaginary scene at the Twentieth CPSU Congress. The script could have been published within the posthumous American edition of *Marxism in Our Time*, but Tamara eventually decided against it. The scene has thus remained in the archives. It is worth quoting at length.

It is the third day of the Congress, 8 p.m. Anastas Mikoyan is addressing the Soviet delegates, who listen with bated breath as he becomes the first to talk disparagingly about the dictator Stalin, the first to cast him as the 'evil genius of the Soviet Union'. Part of the audience receives this as 'a moment of extraordinary mental release', but the rest are completely stupefied, 'as primitive tribesmen might be when they witness unexpectedly the profanation of a tribal taboo—for it consists of tribesmen (sufficiently sophisticated to be ashamed of superstition)'. Mikoyan, speaking under a statue of Lenin, turns his speech to his memory: '[T]he Leninist spirit and Lenin has permeated all our work and decisions, as if Lenin were still alive and here with us! How he would rejoice if he could see us now . . .' Mikoyan wraps it up and moves back to his seat, amid stormy applause, when almost imperceptibly another man, 'very small, with a large bald head, and short but shaggy beard', his thumbs oddly stuck in his waistcoat, takes the rostrum. Nobody notices him at first, no applause greets him; but soon the audience realizes something familiar about him, and eventually notices the striking resemblance between the man and the statue. He begins to talk to them in a voice they have heard a hundred times before on records:

Comrades, I don't very well know how to address you after all these years. I have heard Mikoyan say how very much at home I should have felt among you and how much I would rejoice to see that you are so faithful to my ideas [. . .] How I wish I could confirm to you wholeheartedly what Mikoyan has told you! How I wish I could I tell you that I rejoice in your devotion to what you have chosen to call Leninism! That I truly recognize you in my party, the party I once founded and inspired, and with my comrades' consent led over many years. No, no, no! I would mislead you and cheat you if I told you that [. . .] I have listened to so many speakers here extolling my memory—not one of you has referred to me without describing me as the Great Lenin. What a silly habit this is! How could you, my disciples, succumb, be it even for a moment to so benighted a habit of thought? Have I not sweated enough to teach you to look at the world, and at yourselves, as Marxists? To see the objective laws of development, the relationships of classes and nations and groups within the classes, and to treat leaders as the exponents of class interests and of varied mentalities and ideologies in which the nakedness of class interests is encased, as in so many cocoons? If there was ever any greatness, was it not merely the reflected greatness of our class and of our cause? Have you, for the sake of reflex, forgotten the living reality it reflected, or have you done something far worse? Have you inflicted on me that humiliation and insult of which I had my moments of faint premonition? Have you made me a holy icon? Have you made of me your harmless and ridiculous patron-saint, to whom you burn stinking candles and of whose life you tell incredible tales to credulous children [. . .]? If you have inflicted this insult on me then I declare myself your implacable enemy, and I swear that I shall summon all my might against you! Or do you delude yourselves that I am helpless? You still disseminate my ideas if only because you are the prisoners of your hypocrisy. You cannot use me as your patron saint without publishing and republishing my collected writings, which cannot but set agog the minds of your children, throw them into the most dangerous revolutionary unrest and turn them fully against their hypocritical fathers! Ha-ha-ha! If you have your patron saint, you will be startled to discover that your patron saint is the chief seducer of your children! If you have turned me into a holy icon, then remember that I am a dynamite-laden icon, capable of bursting over your Pharisaical heads [. . .] Tell me the truth, have you made me the object of a sacred ritual? Tell me the truth! [. . .] I must unfortunately take your silence for an answer. How guilt has congealed your faces and your lips! I have yet to see such faces in my party! Or have I perhaps come here by mistake? Are you really the children of the Bolsheviks? I have listened to the man who gave you the report of the mandate commission. He said that among 1,600 delegates to your congress there were twenty-two that had joined our party before the October revolution. Twenty-two! Not more? And what has happened to the rest? Wait, it is now thirty-eight years since we made the revolution. Most of our comrades were very young people. Most joined the party in their teens. Young workers, apprentices and undergraduates from the school bench. The philistines would mock us as the party of immature revolutionaries, of children, but we were proud to be the party of youth, to lead those who were only at the threshold of life and therefore expected from life more than their elders did. Twenty-two! As I look around I can recognize perhaps three, four, five of the faces I once knew. Where are the rest? Have gods loved them all so much as to make them all die so young? [. . .] Is this the Bolshevik Party, I ask you? The party which in my days was divided in opinion even when it united for action—and how it united! The party which perpetually seethed with a ferment of ideas! Will you never heckle your leaders from the floor? Will you never contradict them? Will your rank and file never teach their leaders those severe lessons which our rank and file once taught us? Are you perhaps quite a new species of Bolsheviks, and are those twenty-two old members present here merely the last, amnesia-stricken Mohicans of a destroyed tribe? Open your mouth at last, for the Revolution's sake! Speak! Speak! Speak![1]

Beneath the more comical and rousing moments in this impromptu script, what emerges is a sense of the inexorability of history. For Deutscher, October, 'our revolution', the first proletarian revolution, has atrophied beyond recognition; and at the same time, it cannot be conjured out of existence or regretted. History must be taken as it is, leaving only the hope and the urge of new changes and new breaks in the future.

Deutscher closed his 1965 memo with a wish:

If my work does something to free the minds of a few readers from the fetishes of bourgeois ideology and from the lingering idiocies of Stalinism, I shall have achieved something: and the day in which Russians are free at last to read my *Stalin*, *Trotsky* and *Lenin* will be a great day for me, and perhaps not only for me.

In the event, a version of one of his most important titles, *The Prophet Outcast*, did finally appear in Russian—just months before the fall of the Soviet Union. It is an austere green volume, with some poorly reproduced photographs, entitled *Trotsky in Exile* [*Trotskii v Izgnanii*]. It came out when it was already beyond any doubt that the prospect of democratic reform in the USSR no longer had a prayer.[2] Unlike *Lenin's Childhood*, the *Trotsky* trilogy was fully translated and published in Russian in 2006, just as Putin

1 Deutscher, 'Imaginary Speech by Lenin to the XXth Party Congress', 1956, *IDP* 155.

2 Isaac Deutscher, *Trotskii v Izgnanii*, Moscow, Izdatel'stvo Politicheskoi Literatury, 1991.

was beginning to consolidate his power vertical. In part, then, Deutscher's old wish came true, but at the very time when the worst fetishes of bourgeois ideology were beginning to gel with the revival of the worst Russian authoritarian and imperialist reflexes. Not bad for an irony of history, not only for him.

GONZALO POZO

INTRODUCTION

Isaac Deutscher viewed his planned study of Lenin as the culmination of his life's work. The biography of Stalin, the three volumes on Trotsky, and the life of Lenin were to stand as 'a single essay in a Marxist analysis of the revolution of our age and also a triptych of some artistic unity'. This was not to be. It is all the more grievous because he girded himself for this work very thoroughly for many years. During the research on the Trotsky Archives, in 1950, he had already a mental file of documents and papers which might throw some new light on the chief character of the future volume. The notebooks from the Houghton Library (which houses the Archives) bear here and there the marks of a big L in red pencil; material which had been collected for the Stalin biography bears sometimes a remark: To be consulted for *Lenin*.

When, after 1956, the 'cult of personality' began to be deprecated in Moscow, Lenin's figure assumed a human shape anew: he was no longer the Byzantine saint to be invoked ritualistically by the faithful at every possible opportunity; Russian journals and newspapers were full of reminiscences of former secretaries, collaborators, and even nurses and doctors who, at one time or another, were in contact with Lenin. Then the new fifth edition of Lenin's *Works* appeared in 55 volumes, containing not only Lenin's writings, speeches, letters, and directives but even remarks he had made on the margins of books he had read. All these together with scores and scores of patiently collected rare materials were transferred to the bookshelf nearest to Isaac's desk. They still remain. I can now put before the reader just one fragment, one unfinished chapter, of the work which Isaac Deutscher so passionately desired to complete.

The first chapter of any biography inevitably contains the usual description of family, childhood, and youth; but here the author, delving into the obscure origins of the Ulyanovs, presents a striking picture of the social conditions in which lived the most oppressed, the most backward, and most anonymous of the many nationalities of the extensive and sombre Tsarist Empire.

More interesting than this, however, is the subtle thread which gives the incomplete chapter its unity. We see Ilya Nikolaevich, Lenin's father, who devotes his life to the great cause of education of the benighted muzhiks, wanting to serve the Tsar, the Church, and the People loyally. 'His way of "going to the people", with the Tsar's authority behind him' seems to him the only reasonable course. But he is defeated by autocracy, by the Church, and by reaction, and dies a broken man. Alexander and his friends argue that 'to engage . . . in the elaboration of theoretical principles would amount to surrender. Any philistine can theorize—the revolutionary has to fight.' Alexander and five of his comrades die on the gallows. And yet it was Alexander who maintained that 'it was suicidal to engage in any political activity before one had clarified the principles on which it should be based'. In this respect Vladimir, it seems, started from where his brother, so tragically, was forced to leave off. It was Lenin, the Marxist theoretician, Lenin the philosopher, as well as the leader and the man of action, fallible and great, his whole life completely geared to his purpose, the man who was none the less steeped in theory, who acted within the framework of well-elaborated principles, that Isaac Deutscher sought to portray.

Paraphrasing Carlyle, Isaac said that his job as a

biographer of Trotsky was to drag out his chief character 'from under a mountain of dead dogs, a huge load of calumny and oblivion'. In his biography of Lenin, Isaac, detesting all orthodoxies, conceived his task as that of dragging his chief character from under a huge load of iconography and stifling orthodoxy. Like Mayakovsky, he looked with admiration upon Lenin's 'genuine wise human tremendous brow' and saw in him 'the most earthly of all who have lived on this earth of man'.

TAMARA DEUTSCHER

London, April 1970

LENIN'S CHILDHOOD

The origins of the Ulyanov family are so obscure as to appear enigmatic. Its records go back no further than the first half of the nineteenth century, that is to Lenin's grandfather Nikolai Vassilievich Ulyanov. His descendants described him occasionally as a lower grade civil servant or an office employee domiciled in the city of Astrakhan. For a long time Lenin's biographers accepted this description as accurate and, making it a little neater sociologically, presented the Ulyanovs as a family typical of the Russian working intelligentsia. If this description had been true, the extreme paucity of the information about the Ulyanovs would have been quite inexplicable. Men and women of the Russian intelligentsia were articulate and communicative; they were prolific letter writers and diarists; and, of course, the public archives contained records not only of their careers and social relationships but often also opinions about their political loyalty. Why then was the history of Lenin's ancestors wrapped up in such deep anonymity? This circumstance alone indicates that even two or three generations before Lenin the family must have still been submerged in the peasantry, for only in the peasantry and among the poorest city dwellers had people lived and died—one enslaved nameless and illiterate generation after another —without leaving any written traces of their existence. As the property of their landlords the peasant families had no identity of their own. The serf had his christian name and his patronymic—this much was required for the convenience of the landlord's bailiff and overseer in this world and by the heavenly powers in the next—but he had no right to, and no need of, a family name; and indeed research into the archives of Astrakhan has revealed that about forty years before Lenin's birth the name of the family had not yet been clearly established. Around 1830 the municipal authority had taken just a little notice of the revolutionary's grandfather, but they still referred to him under three different though similar-sounding family names: Ulyanov, Ulyaninov, and Ulyanin. That they were not referring to three different persons is clear, because in all cases the man's first name, patronymic, address, and occupation are the same. Evidently he himself was not yet quite sure how he was called: his name was his most recent acquisition, he was not familiar with its sound, and uncertain of its actual ending. Moreover, the acquisition of the name went hand in hand with the acquisition of an extremely modest piece of property: a small house situated on a sandbank in one of the poorest quarters near the harbour —the fact was recorded in the census of householders of Astrakhan, carried out on 29 January 1835. It is from this document that most of the information about Lenin's grandfather is extracted.

Nikolai Vassilievich Ulyanov was born in 1765. At the time the census was taken, he was seventy. His wife, Anna Alexeevna Smirnov, was twenty-five years his junior. They had four children, two boys and two girls. The oldest, Vassili, was thirteen, the girls Maria and Fedossia were twelve and ten, and the youngest, Ilya, Lenin's future father, was only two. Nikolai Vassilievich's address was given as number 227 'first part of the first quarter'—the anonymity of the street conveys the impression of a drab settlement on the outskirts. The district itself, or part of it, was later renamed Cossack Street, and after the revolution Stepan Razin Street, and the house which still stood there was identified as number 9. The area of which the street formed part was called Kossa—Sandbank—and was in fact a kind of a

lagoon at the bottom of *Zayachyi Gor* or The Hares'
Mound. The district was crowded with hovels of paupers,
poor artisans, and demobilized sailors and soldiers who
settled there after twenty-five years of military service. It
was most unhealthy; only five years before the census, its
population had been decimated by an outbreak of
cholera. Nikolai Vassilievich had bought his house from
F. F. Lipayev, a foreman in a military gun foundry;
and he was paying for it by instalments, so that in 1835
he had not yet acquired the title deeds. But he produced
receipts of the payments,[1] and so authority, though
doubtful about the actual price of the house, consented to
confer upon him the status of a *meshchanin*—a town dweller.

Thus it was only at the age of seventy that Lenin's
grandfather had been officially recognized as a citizen of
Astrakhan. Yet from another document it follows that
he had lived there for fifteen years prior to the census, at
least from the time of his marriage to Anna, the daughter
of Alexei Smirnov. Evidently he then belonged to the
great mass of people who led an existence in and around
the city without possessing the rights of citizenship. Who
were those people?

Astrakhan had once been the capital of Tartar khans
and its native population consisted of Tartars, Kirghizes,
and Kalmuks; only very few were of Russian or Ukrain-
ian stock. The people of Mongol origin were deprived of
all rights. They were treated as a subject race. Russian
noblemen could turn them at will into their serfs, but
this did not, however, occur on a mass scale: on this
outer fringe of the empire, in the desert-like, salty, and
wind-swept wild marshes adjoining the Caspian Sea
there were only a few farming estates and the need for
manpower was limited. All the same, early in the nineteenth century certain forms of slave trade were still
common: Russian merchants were capturing, or buying,

---

[1] The receipts totalled 260 roubles, and the price of the house was 700
roubles.

3

or selling children of Kalmuks and Kirghizes. A law of 1808 required that such children be freed when they reached the age of twenty-five; nearly two decades later enslavement was formally prohibited. A legal document dated 1825 has been brought to light, which instructed a merchant of Astrakhan to release his maid servant Alexandra Ulyanova—a Russian writer suggests that this was a relative of Nikolai Ulyanov, perhaps his sister. If this supposition is correct, then Lenin's grandfather was a Tartar or a Kalmuk, not a Russian. Circumstantial evidence seems to confirm this supposition, not least the fact that Nikolai Ulyanov married the daughter of a Kalmuk. On the other hand, Ulyanov was a member of the Greek Orthodox Church. Was he, like his father-in-law and like a few other Kalmuks or Tartars, a convert to Christianity? No mention of this occurs in any documents known so far. If he was a Russian why and from where did he come to Astrakhan? Only very few Russians lived there at the time, and most of these belonged to the ruling bureaucratic caste or to rich merchant families. Those who belonged to neither were, as a rule, peasants, fugitives from chattel slavery, or ex-serfs who had bought their freedom by paying quit-rent to their former masters.

Astrakhan was attractive because of its remoteness, its openness; it breathed freedom. A fugitive was not likely to be caught there and returned to his landlord. Besides, it was a place where the ex-serf could hope to make a living for this was a time of rapid growth in Astrakhan. As the empire spread southward and eastward, the city became one huge bazaar; and much of Russia's trade with Asia, especially with Persia, went through its harbour, at least until Odessa developed into a dangerous competitor. Astrakhan's merchant families were making fortunes in fishing and caviar, in the import of silk and export of horses, and by monopolizing shipping at the mouth of the Volga. A few of those merchant families had been founded by ex-serfs; and their dazzling success raised the hopes of many others who flocked to the city, assuring it a steady supply of cheap labour. They became stevedores and dockworkers, or learned some craft and settled as independent artisans. Evidently Nikolai Ulyanov was one of them; he was neither civil servant nor office employee, but a tailor. Whether he was his own master or worked for someone else, is not known. He married late in life—when he was fifty-five or older. Did he have, in his younger days, to pay a part of his meagre earnings in quit-rent to his former landlord? Did he have to wait to found a family till the burden of this debt was lifted? In any case, he did not succeed in climbing up, but remained a very poor man all his life. At seventy he had saved just enough to buy, on instalments, the little shack; and to get some additional money he rented the wooden attic to a tenant, living with his wife and children on the ground floor of the house.

He must have been, at seventy, already weary of life when he was officially granted the status of a *meshchanin*. The term, borrowed from Polish where it denoted the burgher or bourgeois, was used in Russia to describe town dwellers of the lower middle classes, petty traders, small property owners who, in accordance with the feudal character of the cities, formed a single estate. Free in comparison with the serfs, they did not enjoy the independence of any European or even Polish burghers. They were subject to corporal punishment and were restricted in their freedom of movement. They had no political rights; although they paid poll tax, they had no vote and were not electors of any representative political or even municipal body. As an estate, they had to supply a certain number of recruits to the army. But they could not hold any posts in the civil service except under a special dispensation of the Tsar or his ministers. In the course of time, as the bureaucratic establishment grew and needed more and more men, this last restriction was to be relaxed; but early in the century it was still rigidly enforced. Thus the peasant who was ambitious enough to climb up from serfdom and to dream of becoming a *meshchanin*, found that after much toil and trouble, when he attained his ambition, he and his children were still at a dead end, and still in bondage.

Lenin's biographer is again and again struck by the extent to which the Ulyanov family was unaware of its social origin. 'I do not know anything about my grandfather', Lenin, as if puzzled by this fact, stated in replying to a questionnaire. His elder sister, Anna Elizarova, imagined their grandfather as a white-collar worker; and they all saw themselves as typical representatives of the intelligentsia. And, indeed, when one views Lenin's parental home and the family life of the youngest son of our Astrakhan tailor, one has the impression of firm middle-class roots and a long established intellectual tradition. It is, of course, common enough for upstarts to conceal their lowly origin. But this was hardly the Ulyanovs' motive. They were remarkably unconcerned about their social status; they took it for granted and were completely at ease with it; they were actually ignorant of their descent. The humble Nikolai Vassilievich died a couple of years after he had been registered as a citizen of Astrakhan; Ilya, his youngest son, was only five or seven years old, and so he grew up without remembering his father, and later on was unable to give his own children any recollections of him. Ilya's elder brother, Vassili, was seventeen when their father died, and he became the family's bread-winner. He had been ambitious to educate himself and rise in the world, but now he had to give up these yearnings. He took employment as a salesman and cart-driver delivering barrels of salt to customers. He devoted himself to the upbringing of his younger brother, for he was determined to achieve for Ilya what he had failed to achieve for himself. He

6

secured an education for Ilya but at the cost of extreme self-denial, by saving every kopek he could lay aside and by remaining a bachelor. A friend of the family, a certain Nikolai Livanov, the *protoyerev* or archpriest of a neighbouring parish and Ilya's godfather, helped by obtaining for the boy a place in the local gymnasium and an occasional donation which covered the school fee. The priest also supervised Ilya's upbringing; and in later years Ilya was to speak with the warmest gratitude of all that his elder brother and the priest had done for him. At this early stage two characteristics of the Ulyanovs are discernible: their strong family ties and their religiousness. Lenin's father was a practising and devout Greek Orthodox Christian to the end of his life and Lenin himself was a believer till he was sixteen. The parish archpriest of Astrakhan undoubtedly left his mark on the antecedents of the greatest and most militant atheist in history. As to the Ulyanovs' strong sense of kinship, this was to survive all the upheavals that affected their ideological outlook.

At the gymnasium Ilya Nikolaevich did extremely well; in 1850, at the age of nineteen, he graduated with a silver medal, the first to be awarded since the school had been founded nearly half a century before. The certificate of graduation contained, however, the emphatic reservation that 'Ulyanov as one who comes from a non-noble estate is not granted hereby any right of entry into the civil service'. To the graduate this restriction was probably a blessing in disguise; it prevented him from embarking upon a low-grade bureaucratic career and induced him to seek entry to the Kazan University. This was a daring ambition, for no pupil of the Astrakhan gymnasium had ever been admitted to the University: academic study too was, in the main, reserved for the children of the upper classes. Undeterred, Ilya Nikolaevich applied for admission as well as for a scholarship. With some difficulty, and only after the

7

director of the Astrakhan gymnasium had backed his application, he was accepted. But he was refused the scholarship, because, as the University's Curator wrote to the director, exhibitions were granted only to officials 'in order to make it easier for them to educate their children. There is no adequate ground . . . for accepting . . . among the exhibitioners . . . Ulyanov who belongs to the lower ("*meshchanskoe*") estate.' But the unfailing Vassili stood by, saving the kopeks and roubles needed to pay the fees; and presently Ilya himself began to earn money by tutoring and coaching children of Kazan merchants.

In the middle of the century Kazan University, the only University in Russia's Eastern provinces, attracted aspiring young men from all the towns on the Volga. It had been founded only recently, at the time of the Napoleonic wars, amid all the intellectual sloth and obscurantism of a backwater. But it had been turned into a great seat of learning by the genius of Nikolai I. Lobachevski, the pioneer of non-Euclidean geometry, who was its Principal for nearly two decades. In 1850, when Ilya Ulyanov was admitted to the faculty of physics and mathematics, Lobachevski was already in retirement; but he still took an interest in the work of promising students. Ilya was one of these. He had a real passion for science and mathematics; despite poor health, he worked hard and wasted no time. In 1854 he graduated and obtained his bachelor's degree on the strength of a thesis on 'Olbers' Method and its Application in Tracing the Comet Klinkerfüss'. A year later he became senior Master of Physics and Mathematics at the Dvoryanski Institute, a school for children of the nobility, at Penza, the chief town of one of the Volga *gubernia*. He was recommended for the post, and the appointment was signed by Lobachevski on whose advice he also took charge of the local meteorological office.

Penza was a dull, somnolent, and caste-ridden

back-water, and its school, maintained by private grants, was anything but an exemplary centre of education. The standards were low; the sons of the nobles were lazy, rowdy, and contemptuous of their masters. The trustees were in arrears with teachers' salaries: in the early 1860s, with the abolition of serfdom, the nobles were stingy with grants and donations and the finances of the school were more shaky than ever. Educational Inspectors reported scathingly on the school's decline, but at least two of them, Senator Safonov who visited the Dvoryanski in 1859 and Inspector Postel who reported on it three years later, remarked on the exceptionally good results —obtained 'thanks to the Master Ulyanov'—in the teaching of mathematics and physics. The young Master was, it seems, equally efficient in running his poorly-equipped meteorological office; he wrote several treatises on meteorology, and a dissertation on storms and lightning conductors, in which he frequently referred to sources in Western European languages. This work, however, added nothing to his earnings—the post at the meteorological office carried no salary.

At Penza, in the home of I. D. Veretennikov, another school master, Ilya Nikolaevich met Maria Alexandrovna Blank, Veretennikov's sister-in-law. He was now about thirty years old, she was four years younger, and by all accounts very handsome and attractive. He fell in love and she responded to his feelings, but they had to delay their marriage, probably because of lack of money, till the summer of 1863. There were in the backgrounds and characters of the young couple certain significant contrasts. She was the daughter of Dr. Alexander Blank, a somewhat enigmatic and eccentric man, of markedly inquisitive mind and restless temperament, who had been influenced by advanced ideas of his time. His name suggests that he was a slightly Russified German or Balt. He had married into a family of Volga Germans, but his wife died young leaving five small daughters and a son.

The orphans were brought up in German language and tradition by a severe aunt. There was also a Swedish aunt and a Swedish grandmother in the family. Thus we find in Lenin's parents the union of two ethnical and cultural extremes, of the South Eastern Asiatic Tartar and the Western Nordic elements with an indefinite Russian-Slavonic admixture. Socially too the two families came from different worlds. Dr. Blank graduated as a physician and surgeon from the Petersburg Medical Academy around 1825, shortly before the Decembrist rising. He had practised as house-physician in hospitals and as forensic doctor in Smolensk, Perm, Riga, and Kazan, but after his wife's death he retired, bought a farm in the village of Kokushkino, near Kazan, and became a small landlord, giving the benefit of his medical knowledge only to his neighbour-villagers. He held curious views on health and education, and to these the upbringing of his own children had to conform strictly. Somewhat of a Rousseauist, he believed in nature healing, in Spartan living, in simple diet and water cures. He probably reacted in this way against the quackery and superstitions of contemporary Russian medicine, but in the process developed his catholicons and nostrums. He denied his children 'the poison' of tea and coffee, and made them drink cold clean water. He denied them also ample and comfortable clothing: they had to expose their bodies to wind, snow, and frost, and to harden them even more, he treated them to frequent cold compresses —the German aunt, it was said, wrapped them in wet cold towels before putting them to bed. We do not know exactly how these experiments affected the health and nerves of all his children; Lenin's mother, at any rate, grew up strong in mind and body and lived, enduring her tragic experiences, to the age of 81. She brought up her children in a Spartan manner too, without however subjecting them to any of the trials she and her sisters and brother had to go through. As to Dr. Blank, though opinionated and somewhat cranky, he gave his children a careful and liberal education. He did not send Maria Alexandrovna to school—he either lacked the money or bowed to the widespread prejudice against sending a girl to a boarding school—but she had her tutors at home, she spoke Russian, German, and French fluently, was widely read in Russian and European literature, loved music, and played the piano with sensitivity and zest. Her cultivated mind was alive with curiosity about the world and eagerness to learn—as a married woman she sat for a teacher's examination and so was well equipped to influence the education of her own children. There were other, still unexplored, intellectual influences at work in the Blank family, for when some years after the doctor's death his grandchildren moved into his rural house, they found there rich collections of radical literary and philosophical journals left behind by an unnamed uncle. In any case, Dr. Blank's home at Kokushkino was culturally poles apart from the hovel of Ulyanov, the Astrakhan tailor. Yet in Lenin his two grandfathers, the plebeian and the intellectual, were to meet and unite.

The Ulyanovs did not remain in Penza for long. Ilya Nikolaevich could not keep a family on the meagre and uncertain income he earned there. The Institute for Children of the Nobility was in a state of utter decay. The pupils were demoralized; there was drunkenness among the boys of the upper forms; they were whipped or expelled or both; in 1862 fifty per cent of the pupils failed at examinations. A few of the masters looked for situations elsewhere. Ilya Nikolaevich obtained a post at the gymnasium in Nizhni Novgorod, where one of his former Astrakhan teachers was headmaster. In 1863 the Ulyanovs moved. They found Nizhnyi Novgorod a far more congenial place than Penza. With its historic background as the stronghold of the Russian merchant class, it was the least caste-ridden and the most civilized of the cities on the Volga, with its own theatre, frequent concerts, and lively literary and debating societies. The gymnasium was a well organized school, well equipped and financially sound. The masters and their families lived in relative comfort in one wing of the school building. The Ulyanovs moved into a four-roomed apartment assigned to them. Ilya Nikolaevich took to teaching with his usual zest, and was extremely active outside the gymnasium as well. He taught at other schools in the town, served on the Council of a military college, occasionally attended teachers' conferences in Moscow, and visited educational exhibitions from which he would return home, thrilled by all he had heard and seen, and loaded with new school aids and new books. He and his wife became popular among teachers and neighbours, and enjoyed social and artistic activities, the closeness to the centres of Russia's intellectual life. Like the rest of the local intelligentsia, they read and discussed the great journals bringing every month the indomitable ideas of a Dobrolyubov or Chernyshevsky and instalments of Tolstoy's *War and Peace*. No wonder that in later times they recalled nostalgically their stay at Nizhnyi.

A year after their arrival their first daughter, Anna, was born, and two years later their son Alexander. They stayed at Nizhnyi just six years. Then, somewhat suddenly, and while Maria Alexandrovna was pregnant with a third child, they left for a new place—Simbirsk. They arrived there in September 1869, and on 10 April 1870 a second son was born to them. Baptized in the little St. Nicolas Church in the new neighbourhood, he was given the name Vladimir. Some writers allude to the symbolic meaning of the name—Vladi-mir signifies 'rule the world'; but the thought of this no more occurred to Lenin's parents than it did to innumerable Russian parents choosing this name for their sons.

At first the child seemed to develop slowly: he was big-headed and top-heavy, bulky and red-faced, started walking late, constantly tumbling down and knocking his head. But soon he made up for this initial slowness and as a toddler was exceptionally vigorous and nimble, a great rascal, full of mischief and a lover of noisy games. He did not play with his toys, says his elder sister, he broke them. At five he could read and write; then for four years or so a parish teacher tutored him at home until he was ready, at the age of nine, to enter the local gymnasium.

To the Ulyanovs the change from Nizhnyi Novgorod to Simbirsk was in many respects sheer loss. Ilya Nikolaevich had accepted the post of Inspector of the primary schools of the Simbirsk *gubernia*. This was an administrative post rather than a teaching job. In consequence of the great reform, and with the beginning of Russia's social modernization, the government set out to increase the network of primary schools, to take them out of the hands of a semi-illiterate clergy, and to place them under the *Zemstvos*, the nobility's new founded organs of self-government. Ilya Nikolaevich was to take charge of this operation in a vast rural and roadless *gubernia*, with nearly a million peasants scattered over hundreds or even thousands of villages and hamlets in 166 *volost* (districts); very few schools existed even in theory and fewer still in reality; children would gather in dilapidated huts to learn from self-taught villagers or only semi-literate priests; peasants and nobles alike distrusted and obstructed any attempt to spread education. His new job took Ilya Nikolaevich away from his home for weeks or months in the country, rushing through heat-wave or snowstorm from *volost* to *volost*, raising funds, searching for people who could be taught to teach, and arguing muzhiks out of their stubborn prejudice against sending children to school. For a family man who was no longer young and whose health was shaky, and for a teacher who loved teaching, this was not, on the face of it, a congenial job. The Ulyanovs' life did not become more abundant and comfortable at Simbirsk; it became less so.

Anna, the eldest daughter, was to recollect that 'mother very painfully felt the change from the lively Nizhnyi Novgorod to this wretched and dull provincial hole, to the poor housing, less civilized conditions, but above all, to the complete loneliness. . . . She would tell us later how sad the first years at Simbirsk were for her. Her only friend was the midwife Ilina, who lived in the same house and assisted at the delivery of all the younger children.' True, there were some compensations for the dreary housing, for Simbirsk was beautifully situated on the high bank of the Volga, amid lush and flowery fields, orchards, and woods covering an immense steep slope, from the top of which there was a magnificent view over the river which in springtime spread in a wide flood and across the endless green plain beyond. Many writers, from Pushkin and Goncharov to Trotsky, have described this rich and colourful landscape. The Ulyanovs moved into an unattractive part of the town: they rented a small apartment in Streletskaya Street, on the so-called Old Crown, a part of the town on the top of the hill, the favourite picnicking place of poor families who lived down below by the river, and climbed up and crowded there on Sundays, leaving behind masses of litter to be blown about by the wind for the rest of the week. The house in Streletskaya Street, where Lenin was born, faced a big jail; from behind its bars prisoners stared at the picnicking crowds.

In the course of the following three years the family changed its home several times; and nearly ten years had to pass before Ilya Nikolaevich could afford to buy a fairly spacious and comfortable wooden house with a garden in Moscow Street, where the family lived until they left Simbirsk.

The loneliness in which the Ulyanovs lived their first years in the town that was to bear their name after Lenin's death, was due to the fact that Simbirsk was the most caste-ridden of all the 'nests of the nobility' on the

Volga. Inherited social divisions were kept up here unyieldingly, and the town's layout reflected them with sharp precision. At the bottom of the slope, on the banks of the Volga, were the slummy, crammed, and smelly quarters of the poor. The houses of the merchants rose up along the slope. On the top, on the New Crown, secluded in parkland and behind high walls, stood the country houses of the nobility; and, again, separated from these and squeezed out to the Old Crown where the Ulyanovs lived, were the homes of the lower civil servants. The estates and castes observed a complicated order of precedence, in accordance with which the holders of the various ranks and titles ranged themselves even in religious processions and at services in the cathedral. Simbirsk was less ancient than most Volgan cities—it had been founded only in the seventeenth century—but its *genius loci* was peculiarly reactionary. This was the rampart against which the great peasant revolt, led by Stenka Razin, broke after its spectacular and victorious progress along the Volga. Hundreds of gallows then darkened the slope above the river. When the peasants rose again, several generations later, under Pugachev, and again overran the land, they did not dare to attack Simbirsk. The city's most famous son, before Lenin, were the historian Karamzin, the most eloquent and chauvinistic apologist of Tsardom and its conquests, and Goncharov, the author of *Oblomov*, who had also been the Governor's secretary and the local censor. The son of a wealthy merchant, and a quasi-liberal conservative, Goncharov depicted in his novel *Obryv (The Slope)*, semi-nostalgically and semi-satirically, the local nobility. But, of course, he immortalized the province in his *Oblomov*, to whom the Simbirsk *gubernia* is what La Mancha had been to Don Quixote. In the character of the nobleman who lazes away his life, unable to summon up enough energy to get out of bed, Goncharov created the symbol of the moral sickness, apathy, and indolence of the Russian landlord, indeed of old Russia at large. Thus, paradoxically, the ex-censor of Simbirsk began to exercise a most powerful revolutionary influence, for his *Oblomov* was crying out for the anti-Oblomov who would come to shake Russia rudely out of her drowsiness and inertia. That anti-Oblomov had just been born in Oblomov's homeland; but to the men of Oblomovka, including Goncharov himself, the old social order was still sacrosanct; it was preserved and protected by the *gubernia*'s remoteness from the capital and by its isolation. Almost to the end of the century Simbirsk had no telegraph, no telephone, and no railway connection with the rest of the world.

The Ulyanovs did not quite fit into local society. Ilya Nikolaevich, the *meshchanin*, despite his new post, held no definite place in social hierarchy; and he was not even a Russian. His job was to carry education to the children of the peasants—but had not Oblomov warned them all that 'literacy is harmful to the muzhik: teach him to read and write and he will stop ploughing'? In other *gubernias* quite a few landlords were modernizing their estates and investing money in industry which needed literate workers. Not so in the Simbirsk province. Here the bigwigs probably still saw something indecent, or even subversive, in the assignment that had brought Ilya Nikolaevich into their town. His relative poverty—so obvious in the choice of a cheaply rented apartment in an inferior quarter, his quite unpretentious behaviour, and the Kalmuk features of his face—all spoke against him. Tartars, Kalmuks, and Chuvashes were unfamiliar here, though there were some around; but their place was at the very bottom of the social pyramid. As to the Ulyanovs, they did not even try to force the barriers that separated them from local society. Ilya Nikolaevich was soon up to his ears in his work, reconnoitring the country and looking at those Potemkin schools listed in official registers but to be found nowhere, attending lessons in the few places where some teaching was done, and assessing educational prospects. He had neither the time nor the inclination to bother about the lack of social contact with the inhabitants of the Old and the New Crowns. We know how Maria Alexandrovna felt: chatting with the next door midwife could hardly relieve her loneliness. She tried to get over it as best she could and became engrossed in running the home and bringing up her children. The family was growing. After two years at Simbirsk she gave birth to her fourth child, Olga; and in 1874 her youngest son, Dimitri, was born. A peasant girl, Varvara Grigorevna, helped her to nurse the infants and became so attached to the family that she was to stay with them till the end of her life. Once or twice the Ulyanovs travelled down the Volga to Astrakhan to show their children to their Kalmuk grandmother and aunts and to Uncle Vassili. But presently the grandmother died; and then some estrangement came about, the visits to Astrakhan ceased, and the children grew up without really knowing the paternal branch of their family.

Maria Alexandrovna preferred to take her children on trips to her family estate at Kokushkino, where every summer Dr. Blank's daughters, all married to professional men, came with their husbands and children for long and jolly holidays. This was Maria Alexandrovna's escape from her loneliness at Simbirsk. Ilya Nikolaevich, too, whatever his affection for his mother, elder brother, and sisters, probably felt more at ease among his wife's kith and kin at Kokushkino than among his own people in the slummy suburb of Astrakhan. There may have been a hint of ingratitude or snobbery in his letting his plebeian family connections lapse in this way. He could hardly help it. His own interests and tastes, not to speak of his wife's yearnings and his desire to bring up their children in a civilized environment, made him behave as he did. The logic of his rise in society imposed itself on his family relationships.

17

After a few years of work in the *gubernia*, Ilya Nikolae-vich was awarded the Order of St. Vladimir and was raised to the ranks of the hereditary nobility with the title of 'Official State Counsellor'. He was also promoted from the post of Inspector to that of Director of the primary schools. His new status in the civil service corresponded to the rank of General: he wore a blue, gold-embroidered uniform, and people were obliged to address him as *Vashe Prevoskhaditelstvo*: Your Excellency.

What, it may be asked, had this plebeian *meshchanin* done to gain this official distinction? How was it related to his attitude to the Tsarist Establishment and to his political views? And how was it to affect his children? Up to the time of his ennoblement, which came to him when he was in his early forties, he had never shown any inclination to rebel against authority. He had never come near any of the revolutionary or radical-liberal circles that exercised an influence on the intelligentsia. He was a faithful servant of the Tsar and a devout Greek Orthodox. Like so many people of humble origin who had risen the hard way, he believed that others could rise similarly and that the social order, such as it was, offered enough scope and opportunity for the lower classes to improve their lot. He distrusted those who condemned Tsardom root and branch and advocated sweeping reforms or revolution. He was convinced that their ideas and actions were blasphemous, that it was a sin to rebel against State and Church, and he did not see how the oppressed could gain anything through disobedience or rebellion. In his young years memories of the suppression of the Decembrist rising were still fresh and forbidding. Then came the terror that crushed the Petrashevsky circle and broke a man of Dostoevsky's stature. After 1848 came the overwhelming defeat of revolution all over Europe, a defeat to which the Tsar's Cossacks made their contribution, and which seemed to rob the radicals of all hope. In the last years of the rule of Nicolas I, while Ulyanov was studying at Kazan University, the spying and persecution of students and teachers assumed such dimensions that every impulse of opposition and radicalism was deadened. All these experiences could only fortify Ilya Nikolaevich Ulyanov in what may be described as the conservatism of a man on the way up, consisting usually, in varying proportions, of a sense of the impotence of rebellion, of a certain gratitude to society, and of fear to risk one's own hard-won career.

Yet Ilya Nikolaevich was not insensitive to the degradation in which the people from whom he had risen were living. All his contemporaries portray him as a humane and warm-hearted man who all his life served the people, according to his lights, idealistically and unstintingly. Though he had climbed the social ladder, he was no climber. There was no trace in him of self-importance. In his gold-embroidered uniform His Excellency was to remain as accessible, modest, and unassuming as ever. He had not smoothed his career by any act of servility. He was the Tsar's loyal servant from a deep, unobtrusive conviction with which his religious faith was bound together; and he believed that he could combine service to the people with his service to the Tsar; indeed, that the two were inseparable. He well knew that Russia was craving for change; he held that the serfs ought to be emancipated, educated, and enabled to enjoy the fruit of their labour; and he had no doubt that the nation at large ought to be allowed to move with the time and express itself freely. He believed in the liberating power of science and technology, and though a fervent member of the Church he had little or nothing in common with the Slavophiles who extolled the spiritual superiority of the native pre-industrial Russian way of life. But he expected the changes and reforms to be promulgated from above, on the Tsar's authority. And when Alexander II, disregarding the opposition of the most reactionary landlords, did indeed proclaim the emancipation of the serfs and initiated reforms in the administration, judiciary, and education, this was to Ilya Nikolaevich a new and glorious dawn. He shared in the national enthusiasm aroused by the Great Reform. He was aware that to some radicals the Tsar's liberalism was suspect, that they treated the Act of Emancipation as a fraud, saying that in freeing the serfs it had robbed them of land and made them again dependent on their former masters. (It was for voicing such criticism that, less than two years later, Chernyshevsky was imprisoned at the Peter-Paul fortress.)

Denunciations of the Reform carried no conviction with Ilya Nikolaevich, who responded with his whole being to the progress that the country was at last making. And so when, in connection with the government's new educational policy, he was offered the post at Simbirsk, he had not a moment's hesitation in exchanging the relative comforts of life at Nizhnyi for the uphill work that awaited him in the backward and God-forsaken *gubernia*: he saw it as his life's mission to carry education to the erstwhile serfs and their children, and he gave himself to this task body and soul. This was his way of paying his debt to the poor and the oppressed. A *Kulturträger*, a pioneer in popular education, he was convinced that education alone would in time offer the remedy to all the evils of Russian society, including those engendered by the Great Reform. The *Kulturträger* could not be a revolutionary, for the harvest of popular education ripens slowly. Ilya Nikolaevich did not look for any of those short cuts through history that were to tempt his children and that his son was so forcefully to open up— he trod patiently through the muddy roads and trackless fields of his *gubernia* to see which promising village boy could be taken to Simbirsk to be trained as a teacher, how many children in one *uyezd* or another were still stranded without any education; and where a school building could be raised. First things came first.

It was about this time—to be precise in 1873—that the great *khozhdenie v narod* was in progress: hundreds of men and women of the intelligentsia 'went out to the people' trying to open the peasants' eyes to the seamy side of the Emancipation and to arouse them against the new forms of their servitude and subjection. It was especially on the peasants of the Simbirsk *gubernia* that these Narodnik propagandists concentrated their efforts. The itinerant Inspector of Schools must have run into some of them as he was making his rounds in the country; it was impossible to miss these well-bred men and women who had come all the way from Petersburg and Moscow and were hectically trying to gain the muzhik's ear. In one sense his and their paths were running parallel, for he too had 'gone out to the people'. But they were moving in opposite directions: he had gone out to the people steadily and confidently with the Tsar's authority behind him; they desperately defied authority. To them he was one of the despicable *chynovniks* (officials) who helped the Tsar and the landlord to keep the peasantry in subjection. To him they were a nine days' wonder which threatened to disturb the country's tranquillity, the tranquillity in which alone his educational work could prosper. Between them, this loyal civil servant and the radical Narodnik, was embodied the central dilemma with which more than one Russian generation was grappling: the dilemma of reform from above and revolution from below.

On the face of it, this was soon settled when the peasants began to chase the Narodnik propagandists from the villages and hand them over to the gendarmes. In 1874, by the time Ilya Nikolaevich was ennobled, the going out to the people, this first significant Narodnik venture, had collapsed: nearly all its participants were in prison. Ilya Nikolaevich could only conclude that his was the sole realistic way of going out to the people; and in a sense he was right. The Narodniks were cruelly disappointed, because the muzhiks believed the Tsar the Emancipator; and when the 'genteel' revolutionaries from the cities began to incite them against the Tsar, they suspected them to be creatures of the former serf-owners, who were trying to sow discord between the people and the Throne. The illusion which the act of emancipation had planted in the mind of the peasantry was not easily to be uprooted; the grandchildren of the serfs were still to cherish it. The Great Reform had postponed the Great Jacquerie for over half a century. To this extent Ilya Nikolaevich's decision to stake everything on reform from above was not devoid of a certain kind of realism.

That his was not an ordinary routine-ridden bureaucratic career and that he was intensely concerned with popular education as a great national issue is clear from the testimonies of his contemporaries written long before the revolution, that is long before Ilya Nikolaevich began to be seen and shown in the reflected glory of his son. When he died the *Simbirske Gubernske Vedomosti—The News of The Simbirsk Gubernia* paid a glowing tribute to his 'warm and sincere love' of his schools and to his 'truly indefatigable and extraordinarily many-sided activity':

Ilya Nikolaevich had to build alone, as it were, the whole educational structure from scratch: to determine the purpose and aim of the teaching, to establish and work out in detail its scale and content, to plan its programme over the years, to choose the textbooks, to show every teacher how to use them and how to apply this or that method of teaching, and in this way to educate the teachers themselves. . . . All this he had to do not in one particular centre, not even in one district, but all over the Simbirsk *gubernia*. And so began Ilya Nikolaevich's tireless journeys into the country, so memorable in our *gubernia*. . . . That his efforts were so extremely successful was due . . . to his ability to deal with people of the most different walks of life, different degree of education, and to his warm-hearted and attractive personality.

The obituary dwelt on 'the rare attentiveness and sympathy' with which the Director treated his subordinates 'never imposing his authority on anyone'. This was not merely the obituarist's *de mortuis nihil nisi bonum*. In 1894, eight years after Ulyanov's death, when it was not very safe to speak well of a man remembered as the father of a would-be regicide, another educationist, V. Nazarev, wrote a series of articles about him in the same newspaper:

> The new Inspector was altogether incapable of being satisfied with a formalistic attitude . . . he was an unusually active and enterprising pedagogue. . . . From his journeys all over the *gubernia* he would come back to town and at once ring the bell at the doors of the chairman and the members of the School Council, shake them up, disturb their peace of mind with alarming reports, telling them that the great majority of our schools existed only on paper, that the masters and mistresses were not even putting in an appearance at the classrooms, that their pupils could neither read nor write nor say the most common prayers. It was quite impossible to put off this restless champion of education . . . he did not hear, and did not want to hear, about anything else except the schools in the Simbirsk *gubernia* entrusted to his care . . . and he bore the incredible weight of this whole work.[1]

The writer relates how Ilya Nikolaevich improvised, from the very beginnings, the training of teachers, himself conducting the courses, until in 1875 he was able to open a Pedagogical Institute at Simbirsk. The students of the Institute, mostly children of peasants, were labelled 'The Ulyanovtsy' even many years later. M. Superansky, the author of a history of education in that part of Russia, wrote in 1906, twenty years after Ulyanov's death: 'Thanks in the main to the energy and extreme devotion of I. N. Ulyanov . . . the teachers who received their training at these courses were our best teachers. . . .' Other memoirists underline Ulyanov's

[1] Out of 683 schools listed in the documents only 460 existed and 80 per cent of these were worthless. *Voprosy Istorii* no. 6, 1967.

simplicity and democratic manner: His Excellency would most often go on his inspections in an uncomfortable *britzska* or in a peasant cart or by train, in the third class compartment, putting a cheap grey coat over his shiny uniform. Others recall his interest and good will towards the non-Russian minorities: he was the first to establish schools for Chuvash and Mordov children and, here again, he himself trained their teachers. One of them became later the director of the Chuvash Teachers' Institute and remained a lifelong friend of the Ulyanov family.

Thus Ilya Nikolaevich was to his children an edifying example of 'service to the people'; he was also accessible to them, friendly, humorous, full of stories and eager for games. Because of his long absences from home, his wife's influence was steadier and perhaps deeper. 'She had her children's love and obedience,' says her eldest daughter, 'she never raised her voice and almost never resorted to punishment.' She had most of the 'German virtues': she was neat and orderly—a perfect housewife—industrious and economical. (Nadezhda Krupskaya, who knew Maria Alexandrovna intimately, was convinced that Lenin inherited from her his organizing ability.) As a married woman and mother, Maria Alexandrovna passed a teacher's examination but she used her pedagogical gifts only with her own children, helping them in their homework. To her they also owed their proficiency in foreign languages—there were days when 'German only' or 'French only' was spoken in the family. (At Nizhnyi she and Ilya Nikolaevich had also learned English.) She also taught them music—she played the piano very well and Volodya was quite a good musician at the age of eight. The Ulyanovs had, however, no feeling for painting or sculpture. They had no pictures in their home, partly perhaps because they could not afford it but in the main because, as their daughter maintains, their sense for visual arts was atrophied; this showed itself even in the indifferent manner in which

24

they furnished their home, which had a severe and puritanical aspect. This indifference to shape and colour was to re-emerge in Lenin whose contempt for decor expressed itself in a ruthless impatience with outward appearances and rose to the height of a distinctive style in revolutionary politics. Lenin, it seems, obtained from his parents all the advantages that the lucky chance of heredity and that upbringing could give him; and he was able to turn even a shortcoming passed on to him into a major advantage.

'We were a friendly and closely-knit family', says one of Lenin's sisters; and all memoirists confirm this. But, of course, the children were aware of open and half-hidden differences of temperament and thinking between the parents: the father was extrovert and ebullient, the mother introvert and reserved. He was at one with his work, *gubernia*, and the Russia he served. She remained detached, having no deep inner connection with their environment. For one thing, she was not Greek Orthodox, though she sometimes described herself as such in official documents and though she accompanied her husband to church. This was the most she could do; she did not share his religious fervour, she did not communicate, nor fast with him. She was more or less indifferent in matters of religion—only in extreme distress, yielding to despair or reverting to a habit acquired in childhood, would she go on her knees and pray in a whisper. Her coolness towards religion sprang from scepticism rather than apathy, and also perhaps from an unavowed distaste for the rites of the Eastern Church. The children never heard the parents arguing about this delicate matter. All the same, the unspoken difference was there like a faint crack in the family's moral cohesion.

Paraphrasing Tolstoy, one may say that unhappy children are unhappy each in his own way, each suffering his own particular misfortune, whereas the happy ones are almost all alike. Volodya's childhood was so happy that it need hardly be described in detail, yet one should perhaps bear in mind this circumstance because it must have contributed to the character of the future revolutionary, to the self-confidence, inner balance, and fullness of his personality. No grave shock and no acute anxiety appears to have upset him up to the age of sixteen. The warmth and discipline of the parental home and the children's little community—there were six of them—provided protection and varied interests, joys, rivalries, and excitement. The reddish, bulky, bouncing Volodya was the noisiest and the most roguish of the children. They called him Kubyshkin—the bellied pot. His closest companion was Olga, only a year and a half younger; he bossed her, ordered her about, and played with her so loudly that the older children could not do their homework; the culprit was shut up in his father's study, made to sit in the 'black chair' until he was ready to behave himself. He went on breaking his toys, impatient to see what was inside them and to satisfy his destructive curiosity. He could be rough, aggressive, and full of mockery; he could tell a lie to conceal a naughty prank, but eventually would return to admit the offence. The 'super ego' in the little boy evidently matched his mischievousness.

One of his favourite games was to set traps for birds, but this came to an end when one of his red-breasted robins died in the cage. In the Red Indians game, his was always the role of the Indian whom the Whites, that is the grown-ups, pursued most savagely and who himself fiercely hunted for wild beasts. He would return from the double hunt and proudly relate his adventures, making the younger children swear that they would not betray him to the Whites. Utterly reckless, he swam through the most dangerous cross-currents in the Volga or the Svyaga or rowed in rotten and leaky boats—on one or two occasions a *burlak* (boatman) hauled him out of the water. He would advance fearlessly into 'haunted places' from which other children kept away, or would steal behind the adults when they went for some nightly escapade through the dark forests. But, above all, he was eager to rival Sasha, who was four years his senior. There was in this rivalry something of the tension between the older and the younger brother which Adlerian psychologists consider important in the formation of character. This rivalry, with its inevitable frustrations, more than anything else provoked his aggressiveness and his sarcasm. Only later, in adolescence, did the nobler element in the emulation subdue the envy.

At the age of nine Volodya entered the local gymnasium, where the headmaster—by a curious freak of history—was Fyodor Mikhailovich Kerensky, the father of Alexander Kerensky[1] whose government was to be overthrown by Lenin's party in 1917. Contrary to what Soviet biographers say about the matter, Kerensky-*père* was to exercise quite a strong influence on Vladimir, much stronger than on Alexander who was also his pupil. Like Ilya Nikolaevich, Fyodor Kerensky was also a rather conservative liberal; over the years the two men became close friends and this fact left some imprint on Lenin's early fortunes.[2]

At school Volodya did extremely well: from the first form to the last he was top of his class. His schoolmates were later to recall that he was extremely attentive, quiet, and orderly during lessons, and the most boisterous and the loudest of them all during breaks. He learned effortlessly and recited his lessons confidently without a hitch.

---

[1] Alexander Kerensky was born in 1881 when Lenin was in the second form of the gymnasium. The scanty reminiscences of Volodya which he gives in his *Memoirs*, published in 1966, are the less credible because the Ulyanovs left Simbirsk when Alexander Kerensky was only six years old.

[2] In the gymnasium the children of the nobility and of the civil servants formed the majority; only one-third came from middle-class homes. As a member of the teaching profession, Ilya Nikolaevich was exempt from paying school fees for his sons. The annual fee amounted to 30 roubles.

'Coming back home', his sister writes,

> Volodya would relate to father what happened at school and how he answered questions. As it was usually the same story of correct answers and good marks, Volodya would rush up . . . through the hall . . . and report hurriedly, without stopping: in Greek five, in German—five. I can still see the scene clearly: I am sitting in father's study and I catch the contented smile which father and mother exchange as their eyes follow the bulky little figure in uniform, with the reddish hair sticking out from under the school cap . . . in Latin—five, in Algebra—five. . . . In those years father would sometimes say to mother that everything was coming to Volodya so easily that he might never acquire the ability to work. . . . His fears proved groundless. . . .

In later years, his sister maintains, Volodya himself became aware of the danger of effortless successes and deliberately forced himself to work. Here his rivalry with Sasha, who was extremely diligent, began to have its beneficial effect. Sasha would remain for hours in his room either reading or doing experiments in chemistry. Chemistry did not appeal to Volodya, but he also stayed in his room and read more and more voraciously. The emulation began to affect his character as well: he tried to assimilate something of Sasha's reserve, discretion, and tact, and to control his own quick temper. But if the ideal—'to be like Sasha'—seemed unattainable, Volodya was at any rate becoming less captious, less derisory, and more appreciative of qualities worthy of imitation. He was doing well at school and very willingly helped less able colleagues; he would often come to the classroom half an hour or so before the lessons started and, standing at the blackboard, act the schoolmaster; quite unselfconsciously he would enjoy the process of teaching. His cousin, Veretennikov, recalls that when on one occasion Volodya, yielding to his satirical turn of mind, brought a simple and timid boy to tears with his mockery, he became contrite and did his best to soothe and console his victim. However, despite all his cheerfulness and jollity, Volodya had no intimate friends among his classmates—perhaps his exceptional ability or his sharp eye and tongue kept them at a distance.

The adolescent was 'the pride of the school', showing a particular bent for the humanities, especially for Latin and Russian literature, which in the upper forms were taught by the headmaster himself. Kerensky was an exacting teacher, laying great stress on clarity and conciseness of expression; he was also able to instil a great love of his subjects in the best pupil. His favourite maxim for the writing of compositions was *non multa sed multum* or 'keep your words tight and your thoughts ample'. Reading Volodya's compositions aloud in the class room, he praised him for the exemplary application of this principle. Latin was Volodya's passion: he translated the most difficult texts *à livre ouvert*; was immersed in Latin classics, and Cicero was his favourite author. Kerensky-*père* was indeed so elated with his pupil that he talked about him to Ulyanov-*père* whenever they met: he had no doubt that Volodya would be a classical scholar of genius. Though this expectation was not to be fulfilled, the good headmaster certainly helped to form the style of the future publicist. (Lenin himself was to tell his wife that Latin was one of those 'dangerous addictions' he had to overcome to do his revolutionary work—the others were music and chess.) His literary interests were stimulated in the family circle where everyone was reciting Pushkin, or Lermontov, or Nekrasov, or, occasionally, Goethe or Shakespeare. Often they would all gather to listen to one of them reading pages from Gogol, Tolstoy, or Turgenev. The characters of their novels remained alive in Volodya's imagination as symbols of various aspects of Russian reality—perhaps none more so than the native Oblomov.

Till the age of sixteen Volodya was religious, though not in his father's fervent and passionate manner. But he took his Greek Orthodox faith and his church-going for granted, as part of an established way of life. He showed no inclination as yet to question the socio-political standards or the moral values accepted by society. To be sure, like all Ulyanovs, he instinctively despised the caste-ridden system which the Great Reform sapped but not destroyed. But the Ulyanovs managed somehow to live as if beyond that system, and, assuming that it was crumbling anyhow, to ignore it. Nothing in the brilliant pupil foreshadowed the revolutionary. There was not even a hint of the rebel about him, not a flicker of that restiveness and not a trace of that 'maladjustment' which marked the adolescence of so many men who later in life settled down quite happily to philistine respectability. He was growing up in almost perfect harmony with his environment. His relatives and schoolmates, some of whom tried later to ante-date his revolutionary development, could not remember a single act of insubordination at school. He had one little row with a disagreeable teacher who had treated an innocent boy unjustly; but when Ilya Nikolaevich remonstrated with Volodya, he promised not to get involved in such incidents any more— and he kept his promise. No wonder that his headmaster was to testify one day that his discipline and political loyalty were as exemplary as his scholarly achievements.

Yet Volodya could not be quite unaware of the grim political drama of those years. He was eleven when Tsar Alexander II was assassinated by the Narodnovoltsy. Services were held in school and in churches; preachers and orators were denouncing the regicides and swearing loyalty to the dynasty. Ilya Nikolaevich was gravely upset. His children remembered in what pensive and sombre mood he received the news of the assassination. He put on his uniform and went out to attend a Mass in the Cathedral, then came home and spoke to his family in deep and bitter anger about the Tsar's assassins. They were, he said, irresponsible criminals who had brought disaster upon Russia. He spoke not merely as a loyal official outraged by subversion. He had grown up in the unrelieved gloom of Nicolas I and the reign of Alexander II was to him a great epoch full of promise: as to almost every muzhik, so to him Alexander was The Emancipator right to the very end. Now he was full of forebodings about the reaction that was bound to set in, a reaction that would link up with the tradition of Nicolas I, and would undo the liberal reforms and the progress of the sixties and seventies. This was, it seems, the only occasion on which Ilya Nikolaevich expressed his political convictions so frankly and bluntly—normally he avoided such talk and let only hints and allusions escape him, for he was wary of arousing in his children any interest in politics. The two older ones, Anna and Alexander, listened—and kept their thoughts to themselves. It was not that they were already in sympathy with the revolutionaries, but that outbursts of conformist indignation, coming from all sides, left them unmoved. Apprehensive about the lack of response from them, Ilya Nikolaevich lapsed into a brooding silence. Volodya had hardly any ideas of his own about the matter, but for the first time he became dimly aware of the importance of the conflicts that were shaking the throne and the country.

The bolt that had struck the Tsar had not flashed out from a cloudless sky. In 1866, after Ilya Nikolaevich left the Dvoryansky Institute at Penza, a former pupil of that school, Dimitri Karakozov, made an attempt on the Tsar's life; then, in the year of Lenin's birth, the country was astir with the Nechaev affair; eight years later Vera Zasulich shot General Trepov, the Governor of St. Petersburg. These shots reverberated even in the Simbirsk backwater. People whispered about the political deportees that had been brought to the town and stayed somewhere down by the river; it was as if Mark Volokhov, the revolutionary character satirized by Goncharov in *Obryv*, or his descendants, had come to life and settled

31

near by. Even the gymnasium had not altogether escaped contamination: in the late seventies a teacher appeared there, a revolutionary, an associate of young Plekhanov, and was alleged to have formed illegal circles among the pupils. But he was soon sacked. Ever since then Kerensky-*père* watched with some anxiety over the loyalty of staff and students. As for Ulyanov-*père*, he did what he could to protect his children from any contact with radical ideas. He was succeeding in this remarkably well as far as Volodya was concerned, but he was failing in 'protecting' the older ones, especially Sasha who ceased to pray, was refusing to attend church, and in the intervals between his scientific experiments was brooding over the writings of Pisarev, Dobrolyubov, and Chernyshevsky. 'When we were in the upper forms', writes Anna,

I read together with Sasha all of Pisarev's works from cover to cover; they had a strong impact on us. These books were banned from libraries, but we borrowed them from an acquaintance, a doctor, who had the complete edition of them. These were the first forbidden books we read. We were so absorbed in them that when we finished the last volume we were deeply saddened to have to part from our beloved author. We walked in the garden and Sasha talked to me about the fate of Pisarev who was drowned—it was said that the gendarme who followed and watched him, saw him disappear in the waves, but deliberately did not call for help and let him die. I was deeply agitated. . . . Sasha, walking by my side, lapsed into his usual silence, only his concentrated and darkened face showed how strong was his emotion also.

Sasha and Anna had by that time become atheists, but they neither entered into any arguments with their parents nor did they try to influence their brother. The difference in age—Sasha was four and Anna was six years older than Volodya—may have accounted to some extent for their behaviour. As Trotsky rightly points out, Sasha and Anna had been formed in the relatively liberal atmosphere of the seventies when the adults talked about politics more freely; in the eighties the parents shunned dangerous topics, and so the younger children grew up less aware of them. Sasha was, in any case, precocious in his political development; Volodya was not. For the time being and for a few years yet Sasha did not belong to any radical circle or show any interest in clandestine politics. He had made up his mind to devote himself to science—and on it all his thoughts and ambitions centred. In 1883 he passed his final examinations with top marks and a gold medal—he too had been the first pupil in his class, though his ability was less conspicuous than Volodya's. His parents, it would seem, had no cause to worry about his future. Yet Ilya Nikolaevich was apprehensive. He sensed intuitively the high moral tension in the boy and its perilous potentialities; and so when in September Sasha was leaving home to enter the University at St. Petersburg, Ilya Nikolaevich implored him to 'take care of himself' and avoid any political entanglements. Sasha promised to do so and he meant to keep his word. He was thrilled by the prospect of studying under Mendeleev, whose Periodical Law had just revolutionized chemistry. In any case, at this particular time the pull of clandestine activity was very feeble indeed. The *Narodnaya Volya*, having exhausted itself in the great terroristic act of 1881, had ceased to exist, and efforts to resuscitate it proved vain: those who had made these efforts, Vera Figner and Lopatin, had just fallen into the hands of the police.

And yet the first letter that Sasha wrote home on 27 September contained an omen. He had arrived in St. Petersburg shortly after Turgenev's death; the body had just been brought from France and the intelligentsia of the capital was preparing to pay its last homage to the writer. 'To-day was Turgenev's funeral', Sasha informed his parents. 'We went with Anna and saw the procession: a mass of wreaths and of people and the coffin under a golden canopy covered with flowers and garlands. But it

33

was impossible to enter the cemetery [the police barred access]. Those who were there said that only four funeral orations were made [the speakers were: the Principal of St. Petersburg University, a liberal-conservative Professor from Moscow, and two relatively unimportant men of letters]. No one else was permitted to speak.' Sasha related the incident briefly, in the last passage of his letter, after he had described in detail how he settled down in St. Petersburg, what room he had taken, and what the rent was, where he was having his meals and how many kopeks each meal cost; he expressed no opinion on what had happened at the funeral. Yet his laconic sentence: 'no one else was permitted to speak' was obviously laden with emotion. Turgenev had been the Ulyanovs' favourite author; his stories had so often been read aloud when the family gathered together; they all delighted in the narrative and style.

For Anna and Sasha to attend Turgenev's funeral was only natural—there was not a hint of 'subversion' in this. Ilya Nikolaevich himself might well have accompanied his children to the Volkovo cemetery had he been in St. Petersburg. Turgenev, it should be remarked, had not been a revolutionary—had he not said that the Venus de Milo aroused in him fewer doubts than did the principles of the French Revolution? He had, as a liberal, quarrelled with the Radicals. Why then, Sasha and Anna must have wondered, had the government been so frightened by the homage paid to him, and why had they behaved with such stupidity and meanness? This question was to recur in the next few months on similar occasions, to call for an answer, and to stimulate Sasha to action. Let us only note in passing that it was at the Volkovo cemetery that the police had held back the crowd that followed Turgenev's coffin. Was there something of a portent in this? Three years later similar events occurring at the same cemetery were to give Sasha the final impulse towards his brief and tragic revolutionary struggle.

As yet the incident of 27 September had no sequel. Sasha was completely absorbed in his academic course; in his letters home he expressed satisfaction with his professors whom he found inspiring lecturers, and with the University's well-equipped laboratories and well-stocked libraries. His scientific interests widened to include zoology and biology as well as chemistry. He wrote home rarely, and his letters were so brief and 'dry'—he described mainly the external circumstances of his daily life—that it was impossible to guess his feelings. His tongue-tied love showed itself only in a few details: he was sending home periodicals in which Ilya Nikolaevich was interested; ferreted through bookstalls to find music which Olga wished to have or cheap editions of Tolstoy's works; and regularly supplied Volodya with books that might be useful for him: 'I am sending Papa the pamphlet on "Mathematical Sophisms" he wanted to have; I think it would be good if Volodya tried to solve these sophisms by himself. Did he receive the German translations I sent him?'[1]

It was evident enough that he led a solitary life. 'I am in good health', runs a typical excerpt from one of his letters, 'I am living as before, working in the laboratory until six o'clock. The evenings I spend mostly at home.' He had hardly any friends—Anna, who also studied in St. Petersburg, was his close companion, but even to her he did not open up; he jealously guarded his privacy in a manner quite unusual for a Russian student. True, he belonged to a *Zemlyachestvo*, a kind of a Friendly Society of students coming from the same province (or town); he was even elected to the Council of those Societies which were the only student organizations the government still tolerated. No doubt, under the cover of these basically non-political mutual aid associations there existed a few semi-clandestine debating circles; Sasha kept aloof from these and deprecated their 'interminable

[1] *Voprosy Istorii KPSS*, no. 5, 1966.

35

empty chatter'. His solitary and uncommunicative ways had as yet nothing in common with the secretiveness of a revolutionary working underground; they merely suited his stern, ascetic character and his concentration on science. He denied himself the simplest pleasures, and, taking all his meals in students' canteens, was spending only part of the allowance his father paid him; coming back home he quietly returned the roubles he had managed to save. During the holidays at Kokushkino he would shut himself in a spare dilapidated kitchen which he turned into a laboratory. The parents worried about his health for he looked pale and weak and tried to get him out of the fumes of his 'laboratory' and make him take part in open air games and country walks. Ilya Nikolaevich liked to tease him as 'our philosopher' or 'our explorer'; Sasha yielded reluctantly, but soon returned to his experiments.

While the fear that Sasha might rebel against authority and thus bring himself and the family into trouble appeared so far to be groundless, Ilya Nikolaevich was nevertheless struck by a political blow of a different kind. Some time in 1884 the Ministry of Education informed him that in the next year he would have to retire from his post. He himself was, as a liberal, in semi-disgrace, and his activity in the *gubernia* was under threat from above.[1] He was only fifty-three years old, and he expected to remain active till the age of sixty. But the Ministry was about to put an end to the semi-liberal educational policy it had initiated under Alexander II. The new Tsar had decided that the children of the lower

[1] The memoirists of the Ulyanov family maintain that 'when Ilya Nikolaevich had behind him twenty-five years of service, the Ministry did not grant him more than one additional year, whereas the majority of high officials were normally granted five more years'. Yet in 1884 Ilya Nikolaevich did not have twenty-five years of service behind him: it was nearly thirty years since he had taken his first teaching job in a private school at Penza, and just a little over twenty since he moved to Kazan, but only fifteen since he entered governmental service at Simbirsk.

classes were receiving more education than was good for autocracy; he did not wish to see any more elementary schools established in the country. Responsibility for existing schools was to be transferred from the relatively enlightened *Zemstvos* to the parishes and priests, who had controlled elementary education before the reforms of the sixties. The teaching programmes were to be drastically curtailed so that the schools should not instil into the peasant children an excessive capacity to think. This counter-reform was part and parcel of a general reaction against the semi-liberal era. The feudal and the most backward elements among the land-owning aristocracy were making a determined effort to regain absolute dominance over the peasantry and to eradicate the spirit of European, that is of bourgeois, progress that had been abroad in state and society for nearly a quarter of a century. They had found an ally in the new Tsar, who was easily persuaded that Alexander II had fallen victim to his own liberalism and they incited him to revenge himself for the dynasty's humiliation and to rule with a mailed fist. The Tsar's chief adviser, K. P. Pobedonostsev, who was also the Procurator of the Holy Synod, exclaimed at the Council of Ministers:

This may be the *finis Russiae*. . . . There are some people who would like us to introduce a constitution . . . a falsehood which . . . as Western Europe shows us, is the tool of every untruth . . . [this would be] our misfortune and our perdition . . .—Russia has been strong thanks to autocracy . . . and they propose to set up a talking shop, something like the French States General. Even now we are suffering from having too many talking shops, which are only under the influence of ignominous and worthless journals, inflaming the popular passions.

The *Zemstvos* and the Municipalities, led by 'immoral and dissolute people', were such 'talking shops';

so were the courts—the lawyers' talking shops—and it was because of them that the most terrible crimes were left unpunished; and now they have given freedom to the press, this most horrible of all 'talking shops'. And that great and sacred idea of the emancipation of the peasants—what has it led to? . . . the peasants have been given freedom, but no proper authority has been established over them; yet without such authority the mass of benighted people cannot live.

Of course, it was too late to re-establish fully-fledged serfdom, for this was incompatible with the growth of capitalist economy; and the risk of a peasant war was too grave. A semi-restoration of serfdom was nevertheless forced through. The peasants were tied to their jobs, and landlords were once again free to flog them to their hearts' content. The 'talking shops' were silenced. The Tsar's governors and the police regained control of the judiciary. The Universities were robbed of all autonomy: henceforth the Ministry appointed Principals and Professors. Student organizations, the Friendly Societies of the *Zemlyachestvos*, were banned. 'Subversive' literature, the works of even the mildest liberal authors—Russian and western European—were removed from the libraries. The pernicious ferment of ideas which had been slowly transforming Russia was to be brought to an end. The intelligentsia was to bow without murmur to autocracy, Orthodoxy, Great Russian chauvinism, and Pan-Slavism.

Thus, all the hopes on which Ilya Nikolaevich had based his life and work were shattered; and his conviction that he could 'loyally serve the Tsar *and* the people' had turned out to be a pathetic fallacy. It was ten years since the failure of the Narodniks to arouse the peasants had confirmed him in his belief that his way of 'going to the people', with the Tsar's authority behind him, was the only reasonable one. Now he was defeated far more thoroughly than they had been, for they had at least acted as pioneers of revolution whose failure turned the minds of their successors towards other methods of revolutionary struggle, whereas he, the liberal-conservative civil servant, had reached a dead end. Ilya Nikolaevich may not have been quite aware of this, but he felt defeat in his bones. He probably still blamed the revolutionaries for having provoked the present reaction—he could not see that they represented a historic necessity far larger than themselves. Yet even their 'excesses' could not justify in his eyes a recourse to so crude, vicious, and barbaric a repression, and he could make no peace with it. He himself was too deeply hurt for this. During his fifteen years at Simbirsk he had founded 450 new schools; and the number of pupils in the *gubernia* had doubled. And now he was given to understand that this work, into which he had put all his heart and mind, was unwelcome and that he would have nothing more to do with his schools. He had also, of course, private reasons for anxiety: the prospect of inactivity terrified him; and he was worried about his family's insecurity—he had no financial resources and his pension was going to be inadequate. True, his friends were still trying to persuade the Ministry that he should be left in his post. But it was to take the Minister a year to make up his mind, and for Ilya Nikolaevich this was a year of strain and mortification. When a favourable decision came through at last—the Minister eventually confirmed him in service for another five years—Ilya Nikolaevich was already a broken man. And, in any case, the Ministry's decision offered him only meagre consolation: it was just as humiliating for him to go on serving in the new circumstances as it was to be dismissed. The government's policy left no scope for the liberal educationist and all he could do now was to preside in impotence over the triumph of obscurantism engulfing the schools that were his creation.

Ilya Nikolaevich tried to conceal his feelings from his children. 'Only later did I understand', writes Anna, 'how much distress all this gave to father and how it hastened for him the fatal *dénouement*.' She describes how in 1885, travelling home from St. Petersburg for her

39

Christmas holidays, she alighted in Syzran, the last railway station on the way to Simbirsk, and there met her father who was returning on horseback from what was to be his last inspection of the *gubernia*. In her description he looked somewhat like Don Quixote, riding home for the last time, defeated and clear-sighted after all his battles and peregrinations. There was no trace left of his ebullience and optimism.

I remember that I was at once struck by the impression that father had strongly aged and that he was much weaker than he had been in the autumn—this was less than a month before his death. I remember also that he was strangely despondent: he was telling me brokenheartedly that the government was now inclined to build only church and parish schools and to replace with these the Zemstvo schools. This meant that the whole work of his life was blotted out.

The collapse of his hopes was made even more evident to Ilya Nikolaevich by Sasha's letters in which he described how the iron hand was gripping the Universities. After the disbandment of the *Zemlyachestvos*, students were threatened with expulsion from the University for having belonged to them. Sasha sensed that his father was worrying, especially as the newspapers were reporting troubles in Kiev and Moscow, where students protested against the new rules and regulations. He hastened to reassure Ilya Nikolaevich: 'You are probably anxious as you read about the disorders at the Kiev and Moscow Universities. Here things are still quiet. . . .' But even these words were ominous in their suggestiveness that trouble might be brewing in St. Petersburg too. From time to time Sasha reported briefly on the dismissals or resignations of professors and lecturers who were suspected of being opposed to Pobedonostsev's ideas, especially to official Pan-Slavism. One of them was F. M. Dimitriev, a historian of Russian law, who had been a colleague and, it seems, a friend of Ilya Nikolaevich at Simbirsk. Sasha was still 'taking care of himself' and was not expressing any opinion of his own, except that occasionally he would remark that one or another dismissed man was 'a very good professor indeed'. For all their restraint, these communications were part of an argument between father and son, an argument conducted in hints and suggestions. Sasha's views were still far from crystallized; yet every letter showed him as siding with those who were in conflict with authority. Ilya Nikolaevich could only vaguely guess in which direction his son's thoughts and feelings were drifting, and he had no arguments left to arrest the drift.

It was in this depressed mood that Ilya Nikolaevich spent the last weeks and days of his life. The end of December and the whole of January were as always filled for him with feverish work on preparation of the annual reports. A colleague, V. Nazarev, remembers that 'at the beginning of January 1886 he worked from morning till night on his complicated report' and 'on 12 January at 3 p.m., wearied by his work, he willy-nilly put away the pen. . . .' For some days already he had felt ill; no one suspected, however, that this was more than a temporary indisposition. 'Sufficient attention was not given to the illness; father was on his feet, continued to work and was being visited by his co-workers—other school Inspectors. On 12 January he could hardly sleep at all. I was by his side and he asked me to read out to him some documents. But I noticed that he was getting a little confused and that his tongue was faltering and I persuaded him to stop the reading.' Next day he did not join the family at table, saying that he had no appetite; but he 'came to the door and looked at us ("just as if he had come to say goodbye" —mother said later). He went to lie down on the sofa in his study . . . at about five o'clock mother called me and Volodya in alarm. It was evident that father was dying. He shuddered several times, and became quite still.' He was only fifty-five and, according to medical opinion, his death had been caused by a haemorrhage of the brain—

Lenin was to die of the same cause at fifty-four. Somewhat vaguely his daughter Anna suggests that his illness was probably a disease of the brain and had not been rightly diagnosed; but she also maintained that the psychological and nervous strain to which Ilya Nikolaevich had been subjected speeded up his death. (The same pattern of moral strain and illness was to characterize the last period of Lenin's life too.)

The funeral was arranged with all the pomp and ceremony due to the rank of the deceased, with all the Greek Orthodox abundance of lamentation and incense. V. V. Kashkadamova, a family friend and tutor to the Ulyanovs' children, recalls that the house was full of people and that Mitya (Dimitri), the Ulyanovs' youngest child whom the adults had tried to keep away from the tumult, came running and shouted excitedly: 'This is the fifth service for the dead they are holding here to-day.' Maria Alexandrovna stood by the coffin 'pale, calm, without tears or plaintiveness'. According to the *Simbirske Gubernske Vedomosti,* 'an immense crowd' had filled the street outside Ulyanov's home when the coffin 'was carried out by the second son (Vladimir) and the closest colleagues and friends of the deceased'. (It was probably the first time that a newspaper report spoke about the future Lenin.) At the cemetery, within the enclosure of the Pokrovsky Friary, there was no end to the dirges and funeral speeches; and the grave was covered with garlands and wreaths carrying inscriptions such as this: 'From the Parish teachers of the city of Simbirsk struck by the premature loss of a leader and father.' In descriptions of the scene at the cemetery there stands out the silent and dry-eyed figure of the widow who, as Kashkadamova remarks, 'withdrew into herself, turned away from society and acquaintances, and devoted herself even more intensely to her family'. The harsh realities of her widowhood forced themselves on her attention at once. Ilya Nikolaevich had left his family penniless; even on the day before the funeral she had to apply for a pension for herself and her 'four small children'. When more than three months passed without her receiving any answer, she applied again to 'His Excellency the Trustee of the Kazan Educational District, the Confidential Counsellor Porfiry Nikolaevich Maslennikov', writing:

My husband, Ilya Nikolaevich Ulyanov, was in the educational service for over thirty years . . . he died and I have been left without means, with four small children attending school and two more studying at higher academic establishments. I have to support them all. Although my husband was entitled to a pension, I have not been receiving it yet, and so I allow myself to ask you most respectfully whether it would not be possible for me to receive a single relief payment.

A week later she reiterated her 'humble request', saying that it would probably take time before she was accorded the pension, but in the meantime she had to live,

to pay back the money borrowed for the husband's funeral, to maintain the children, to keep a daughter who was studying at the Pedagogical courses in Petersburg and an older son who had graduated from the Simbirsk gymnasium with a golden medal and is now in his third year at the Science Faculty of the University of Petersburg, where he works successfully and has just been awarded a gold medal for the thesis he had presented. I hope that, with God's help, he will in the future become a support for me and his younger brothers and sisters, but for the present he and the other children still need my help. . . .

Eventually she and the children were jointly granted an annual pension of 1200 roubles. This was not enough to cover the family's expenses and so Maria Alexandrovna rented half of her house to various tenants.

Vladimir was nearly sixteen at his father's death; he was the oldest of the Ulyanov children at Simbirsk. Sasha had not come to the funeral. The news reached him after some delay, and he was just preparing for the examinations as a result of which he was awarded that Gold Medal which Maria Alexandrovna had mentioned

43

with such pride in her petition to the educational author-ities.[1] Some biographers see in his absence a sign of an estrangement from his family; one or two memoirists on the other hand recall how badly shaken and depressed he was by his father's death and how after a week or so he outwardly regained control of himself and took up his work. Anna stayed in Simbirsk for two months, but at her mother's insistence returned to St. Petersburg to continue her studies. And so Volodya had to act *in loco parentis*. But the family's misfortune did not otherwise disturb his buoyant adolescence. On the contrary, the disappearance of paternal authority released him from inhibitions and he became even more self-assertive than he had been. 'Volodya', says his sister Anna, 'was in that age of transition when boys are especially rude and aggressive. This became even more apparent in him— who had always been rather rough and self-confident— now that his father was no more. . . . I remember how disturbing to me was Volodya's harshness of behaviour.'

In the summer there was the usual family reunion first at Simbirsk and then at Kokushkino—this was the last summer Sasha was to spend with them all. He was with-drawn and, as usual, he would shut himself in the 'laboratory' or become engrossed in a book about which no one in the family had ever heard before: *Das Kapital* by Karl Marx. In spite of Sasha's aloofness every one noticed also a certain estrangement between him and Vladimir. Anna relates that she once asked directly Sasha's opinion of his younger brother: 'No doubt he is a very able young man, but we do not get along well (or he might have said: we do not get along at all)—I do not remember the exact nuance, but I remember that he said this firmly and decisively.' Sasha was not inclined to say anything more on the subject, but Anna remarks that 'Volodya's scorn, disrespect, especially towards the

[1] Alexander's thesis which earned him the distinction dealt with 'the segmentary and reproductive organs of fresh water Annelides'.

mother whom he began to answer back as he would have never dared when father was alive—his impertinence and sarcasm . . . were absolutely alien to [Sasha] . . . who reacted to them sorely. . . .' And yet young Vladimir had immense respect for his older brother and since childhood had tried to imitate him. Was his intractable behaviour a kind of compensation for the awareness that his ideal was still beyond his reach? Was his self-assertiveness only the other side of the shield which protected him from utter frustration?

For Sasha this was a fateful year. He was in graver mood than he used to be, and Volodya's pranks irritated him even more. Sasha, too, was now, after father's death, freed from certain inhibitions but in a manner peculiar to him. His mind turned decisively from purely scientific preoccupations to social affairs and to politics. He could no longer escape from the stifling air of all-pervading obscurantism and terror into the university's lecture halls and laboratories. Barely a fortnight after he had concluded his thesis on the characteristics of fresh water Annelides, he became involved, on 19 February, in a political event of considerable significance: he was one of the organizers of a student demonstration called to commemorate the champions of the Great Reform on its twenty-fifth anniversary. As Trotsky points out, the purpose of the demonstration was extremely modest in itself. The Great Reform had, after all, been denounced by the Narodniks and the Narodnovoltsy and by all the radicals as a half-measure and as a fraud. Until quite recently only conservative-liberals have seen in it a milestone on the road of progress or an epoch-making event. The mere fact that a new generation of students was ready to celebrate it and to glorify it as such reflected only a steep decline from the high level of social criticism and political aspirations of the 1860s and 1870s. However, amid the vicious reaction against the era of the Great Reform which marked the rule of Alexander III, the students'

45

plan appeared an act of extreme opposition to the government. Everyone saw it in this light: the students who were eager to break the oppressive silence that reigned in St. Petersburg; the conservatives who were trying to undo the Reform; and the Tsar himself who saw the hydra of regicide rearing its head in the pretence of paying tribute to his father's rule. The students did not in fact call for any mass meeting or street demonstration; they planned to hold a commemorative service at the Volkovo cemetery, the scene of Turgenev's funeral nearly three years earlier. Once again, Alexander Ulyanov did not have to be a revolutionary, or even an ultra-radical, to feel attracted by the idea—only a few years earlier even his father might have wished to participate in a tribute to the champions of the Great Reform. The transition from moderate liberalism to radicalism, and from radicalism to revolutionary action was occurring in a logical but almost imperceptible sequence.

On 19 February there were about four hundred students at the cemetery; but once again they were forestalled by the police and the gendarmerie who, massed in force, barred the way. The students were indignant; the government was alerted. The authorities, having suppressed all student organizations, could not find out where the impulse for the action had originated and who were its initiators; they came to the conclusion that the suppression was not thorough enough. Early in April, the Chief of Police of the capital ordered all students' canteens to be closed; where if not at these cheap eating places had the 'lean, hungry, savage, anti-everything' met and conspired?[1] These reprisals, ludicrous though they were, had their effect: the malcontents found it more difficult to communicate with one another, and the bolder spirits were cut off from the great mass of the intimidated and fearful. However, within the small circle to which Alexander became drawn almost in spite of

[1] Sasha reported this fact in his letter home dated 7 April 1886.

46

himself, exasperation stimulated radical political thinking —it was not by chance that this very summer he was to bring with him to Kokushkino a copy of *Das Kapital*.

It was not easy to get hold of Marx's writings in the St. Petersburg of these years. However, a trusted customer could buy a copy under the counter, as it were, from a small second-hand book dealer. Plekhanov's *Socialism and Political Struggle* or his *Our Controversies*, published abroad only a couple of years earlier, could also be obtained in this way or borrowed from a fellow student; and Sasha had read at least one of these either before his summer holiday or shortly after. Plekhanov was drawing a new perspective for the struggle in Russia: he exploded Narodnik illusions about peasant socialism, and although he criticized severely the Narodnovoltsy with whom he had broken, he nevertheless paid tribute to their understanding of the need for a political struggle against the autocratic system; and he concluded, of course, with his prediction that in Russia too the industrial working class would be the chief driving force of the coming revolution. Among the few students with whom Alexander could discuss these matters some were already describing themselves as Social Democrats and Plekhanovists, while others were still harking back to the Narodniks or the Narodnovoltsy. Alexander seems to have been grappling with these problems and, impressed by Plekhanov's insistence that Marxian theory was applicable to Russia as well as to Western Europe, decided to study the theory at its source. There is no doubt that *Das Kapital* made on him an overwhelming impact. He discussed it with Anna and later with his comrades. But the effect on him of Marx's and Plekhanov's ideas was in a sense only negative. He lost his illusions about the efficacy of the Narodniks; he saw that the conception of a socialism based on the village commune was unrealistic; that the autocratic system in Russia could not be overthrown by a few terroristic attempts on the Tsar; he did not see how

47

Marx's theory or Plekhanov's reasoning could be translated into action immediately. The prospect of a revolution that was to be carried out by the industrial working class was all too distant. Russia's industrialization was only just beginning and the few factory workers to be found in St. Petersburg or elsewhere were not yet able to play any part in the nation's political life, even though some individuals among them were already attracted to socialism and staged a strike here and there. The peasants, in hopelessness and helplessness, were enduring the semi-restoration of serfdom; the intelligentsia, that is those among them who were not simply following Pobedonostsev and the Pan-Slavists, were devoid of any political aspiration, terrorized and demoralized by all the failures of the radical movements. The autocratic system had become unendurable, yet no class in society was capable of challenging it, let alone of destroying it.

Such were the clearsighted conclusions which the young man—he was just twenty—had reached after his discussions in St. Petersburg and his brooding over *Das Kapital* in the summer. He was to state these ideas with cruel lucidity only a few months later, from the dock. He knew that the nation was politically in an impasse; that nothing could be done for the time being to change this state of affairs, nothing except to work for the future by spreading new ideas abroad, as Plekhanov was doing; he knew that revolutionaries trying to resume the struggle inside Russia were doomed to defeat. To him nothing was left but to put aside the insoluble political dilemmas and to return to academic work. Mendeleev's ideas could be further developed and put to use in Russia regardless of the autocratic regime—Marx's could not. Alexander's gloomy frame of mind during his last summer with the family seems to have been due to his inner shrinking from revolutionary action and not, as his sister supposes, from his decision to plunge into it. This was probably the reason for the extreme reticence, 'unusual even for him', which she noticed; less than ever before did he communicate his political thoughts even to her, of whose sympathy and understanding he could be quite confident. It is not in the nature of a revolutionary to confide in anyone his sense of impasse and his dejection. Had he arrived at other, more hopeful, conclusions, he would hardly have failed to share them with Anna. Nor did he make the slightest attempt to influence Volodya.

During this summer, because of restricted circumstances, the brothers shared a room; while Sasha was poring over *Das Kapital*, Volodya, lying on a couch, read and re-read all of Turgenev's novels, went into raptures over them, but showed not the slightest interest in the book in which his brother was so deeply absorbed. Volodya often visited his school friend, Apolon Apolonovich, the son of a wealthy and noble landowner who had a large library. Volodya would climb to its upper shelves, and seated on top of a small ladder would read and read endlessly. Returning home he brimmed over with enthusiasm for all he had just read. His mind was given to poetry and fiction—nothing else mattered. Sasha never tried to awaken in him any interest in economics or in politics, though nothing would have been more natural for a fervent and hopeful revolutionary. The difference of age between them no longer mattered—the 'exceptionally able' adolescent of sixteen would have certainly been intelligent enough to grasp something of the ideas that were preoccupying his brother. He was at this time mature enough to coach his sister Anna, so much older than him, in Latin, which she needed for her examination, and to show her that the curriculum for which eight years were normally allowed at the gymnasium could be done, when taught rationally, within a year or two. He was also giving regular lessons to a teacher of the local Chuvash school, a father of a large family, who was preparing to enter University. Surely then the great issues that were at the centre of current radical controversies were not altogether above his understanding? Nor could Sasha's dislike of his brother's temper and manners account for his withdrawal and reserve. Volodya's behaviour was, as his sister says, a symptom of adolescent rebelliousness which led him to 'reject' the authority and the moral values of the adult world; he already described himself as an atheist and kept sneering and scoffing at the narrow-mindedness and stupidity of some of his schoolmasters. It is in this state of mind that the young are most open to radical or revolutionary influences; if Sasha refused nevertheless to act as his brother's guide, he did so because he himself was in a quandary and could see no way ahead. What was the use of getting Volodya, or even Anna, involved in social and political affairs if this could lead only to frustration in an impasse? He preferred to conceal from them his own predicament.

Early in the autumn he was back in St. Petersburg, tense, perplexed, and inclined to keep aloof from politics. But he could not turn his back on the circle of radical students with whom he was in sympathy and in whose discussions he was playing an increasingly prominent part —this would have been an act of desertion. In October he was elected secretary of the University's Literary-Scientific Society, which had the blessing of the academic authorities. He was not yet a member of any clandestine organization, and none, it seems, existed at the University. It is therefore not quite clear from whom the initiative came for the next political demonstration, the last in which Alexander was to take part. This, too, was to be nothing more subversive than a commemorative service at the Volkovo cemetery; it was to be held on 17 November on the twenty-fifth anniversary of the death of N. A. Dobrolyubov.

That the young so persistently made their pilgrimages to the burial ground to cry out their craving for a freer life over the graves of the fighters of the past, and that the Volkovo cemetery was the scene of all the three demonstrations in which Alexander Ulyanov appeared, was an eloquent testimony to the depths of the moral and political depression of those years. Yet this commemoration was a far more explicit challenge to the Tsarist establishment and its pseudoliberal allies than the previous ones: Dobrolyubov, whom Marx had described as Russia's Lessing or Diderot, had been a revolutionary, an inspirer of the Narodnik movement, a severe critic of the anaemic Russian liberalism as well as an indomitable enemy of the autocracy. From the tribute to Turgenev in 1883, and the commemoration of the Great Reform in 1886, to the demonstration in honour of Dobrolyubov, a radical political shift had occurred in the thinking of the organizers.

The authorities were aware of this. When a crowd of students considerably larger than ever before—six hundred people according to some sources, a thousand according to others—assembled outside the cemetery they found the gates closed: it was announced that the Chief of the Police himself forbade the holding of the service. On turning back, the students found themselves surrounded by a Cossack detachment, and many were arrested. Forty students were expelled from the University and deported from St. Petersburg. The victimization of such a large number of students who could not even be charged with having committed any legal offence caused great indignation. Their friends felt bound in duty to protest.

Alexander Ulyanov drafted a letter denouncing the reprisals, the ban on the demonstration, and the use of Cossacks against the students. The letter was duplicated and sent out to University professors, well-known writers, editors, and members of the legal profession. Not a single letter, however, reached its destination. The police had managed to intercept them all, which indicated how closely the censorship scrutinized all private correspondence. This drove most of the students to despair. It showed them that even the most limited and cautious appeals to public opinion were futile. The students were unable to make themselves heard at the University where they were not allowed to call a meeting; they had been prevented from using the cemetery as a place of secular worship; and the gendarme had pushed his ubiquitous hand even into the letter boxes and prevented their protest from reaching even the small elite of the intelligentsia.

Some critics, including Trotsky, maintain that the group with which Alexander Ulyanov was associated had made no attempt to voice their ideas and gain the ear of any social class before they embarked on their terroristic conspiracy. This view is not correct, for they had made the attempt repeatedly and each time they were thwarted. All means of communicating with their fellow citizens had been denied them. In this respect their position was far worse than that of the Narodniks and the Narodnovoltsy who had, under Alexander II, enjoyed a certain freedom of movement which, however restricted, allowed them to have some links with the peasants and to influence a section of the intelligentsia. Alexander Ulyanov and his friends worked in conditions not very different from those that had prevailed under the rule of Nicolas I, thirty or thirty-five years earlier, when censorship and the terror silenced effectively the faintest whisper of unauthorized ideas. Under these circumstances conspiracy appeared to the students as the only way out—the alternative was utter passivity. Unable to express their protest from any public platform or even through a private letter, they resolved to voice it in a different manner and to seek resonance for it by means of bomb and revolver.

Alexander Ulyanov was aware that this was a counsel of despair. In the last weeks of the year he still argued against the plot, saying that it was absurd, and even suicidal, to engage in any political activity before one had clarified the principles on which it should be based.

He felt the need for more theoretical work and for a more precise definition of aims and means. This shows him to have been perhaps more mature intellectually than were the other would-be conspirators, though most of them were three or four years his seniors. But they answered his scruples with a telling reproach: are we going to sit back, arms folded, while our colleagues and friends are victimized and while the nation at large is being oppressed and stultified? To engage now, they said, in the elaboration of theoretical principles would amount to surrender. Any philistine can theorize—the revolutionary has to fight. This was, of course, the voice of inexperience and impatience, the voice of youth. Alexander's sense of revolutionary honour was sensitive to it, and against his better knowledge he yielded: no, he would not sit back, his arms folded.

It was already January 1887 when the conspirators formed the clandestine body that undertook to make the attempt on the Tsar's life. Altogether fifteen people participated in the plot: nine students, one graduate of the theological Academy of St. Petersburg, one apothecary, one man of undefined occupation, and three women, two midwives and a schoolmistress. The weakness of the group was so obvious even to its members that they did not pretend to form a new party, but modestly described themselves merely as 'the terrorist section' of the *Narodnaya Volya*. They saw themselves as continuing the work of Andrei Zhelyabov, Sophie Perovskaya, and Nicolai Kibalchich, the assassins of Alexander II.[1] The leader of the group was twenty-four-year-old student Pyotr Shevyrev and its most energetic members were Ulyanov and Osipanov. Two Poles were also involved in the plot: Joseph Lukashevich, a student of geology, and Bronislaw Pilsudski, the brother of the future Polish dictator

---

[1] In the conspiracy of 1881 only thirty-six people took part. But their action had been prepared for much longer and in more favourable circumstances.

Marshal Joseph Pilsudski. One of the organizers, Orest Govorukhin, suspecting that he was shadowed by police, fled abroad even before the 'terrorist section' became organized. Shevyrev and Ulyanov were in some disagreement. Ulyanov demanded a more careful check of the character and credentials of members and was in favour of restricting the circle even further. He was overruled; two of the participants, admitted despite his objections, were later to break down and betray their comrades. It is tempting to see in Alexander's attitude an anticipation of Lenin's restrictive definition of the membership of a clandestine party, the famous Paragraph 1 of the party statutes that was to lead, sixteen years later, to the momentous split between Bolsheviks and Mensheviks. The analogy may be far fetched, for the circumstances in which the two brothers acted and the context in which they argued were vastly different; but it is quite possible that the memories of the tragic collapse of the organization to which Alexander belonged coloured the manner in which his younger brother was to treat the problem of membership of a clandestine party.

The conspirators resolved to kill the Tsar on 1 March 1887, on the sixth anniversary of the assassination of Alexander II. They left themselves less than two months for preparations: any terrorist conspiracy is usually beset by contradictory dangers of hasty improvisation and lengthy arrangements which give the police a greater chance of detecting the plot. Undoubtedly the date of 1 March with its symbolic content fascinated Zhelyabov's successors. But they were short not only of time; they had no experience, no detailed plan of action, no technical resources. They were bound to fail. Ulyanov was full of foreboding but he could not contract out. He was not to participate directly in the assault on the Tsar—Generalov, Andreyushkin, Osipanov and one or two other students were assigned to throw the bombs and fire the shots. But Ulyanov's role was crucial. He drafted the programme that was to explain to the people the purpose of the conspiracy; he was also to manufacture the bombs. The group was penniless—Alexander himself had pawned his gold medal for a hundred roubles so that Govorukhin could go abroad—and they had no means of obtaining the explosives. Weeks passed before Pilsudski was able eventually to bring nitric acid from Vilna and before they managed to buy two second-hand revolvers. The explosives turned out to be too weak; the revolvers did not fire. Just as fatal was the innocence of one of the conspirators who in a letter to a friend in Kharkov let himself go with an exalted, almost dithyrambic justification of revolutionary terrorism. The police intercepted the letter, arrested the addressee, obtained from him the writer's name and began to watch him just before the end of February. On the last day of the month they saw him and his comrades at the Nevski Prospect carrying some parcels. On the next day the police, noticing the same men with their parcels at the same place, arrested them and marched them off to the nearest police station. And so they went, carrying the bombs and revolvers. Little did their captors know what was in the 'parcels'. But at the station one of the conspirators tried to make use of their 'arms': he threw the bomb, but it failed to explode. At the interrogation Kancher and Gorkun revealed the names of other members of 'The Terrorist Section of the *Narodnaya Volya*'.

Alexander was arrested immediately. A search was carried out in his room. Anna, who had not been initiated into the plot and had no inkling of it, was arrested when she came to visit her brother on the very same day. It seems that without any hesitation Alexander made up his mind to take upon himself the whole burden of responsibility and to save as many of his comrades as he could. At the preliminary interrogation he said what he was to state later at the trial: 'I was one of the first who had the idea of forming a terrorist group and I played the most active part in its organization. . . .' 'As to my moral and intellectual commitment in this affair—that has been complete. I have given to it all my ability, all my knowledge, and all the force of my convictions.' He had no illusions about his fate: 'I wanted to kill a man—that means that now I may be killed', he said during one of his last meetings with his mother. At the trial he was concerned only with stating as clearly as possible the case against the Tsar and the government. It so happened that the text of the programme he had drafted on behalf of the group went astray and so this piece of evidence was missing from the prosecutor's file. Alexander rewrote the document in his cell and handed it to the court. He proudly upheld his ideas and exposed with the utmost precision the compelling circumstances that had forced him and his comrades to act as they did. He denounced autocracy as the nation's enemy and proclaimed the revolutionary's right and duty to use every means available to overthrow it. With clearsighted passion he embraced his martyrdom.

It took a few days for the news of Alexander's and Anna's arrest to reach Simbirsk. A relative of the Blank family informed Kashkadamova asking her to break the news to the mother. Kashkadamova seemed to have lacked the courage; she got in touch with Volodya who came straight from school. He read the letter from St. Petersburg in concentration and silence: 'In front of me there sat no longer a heedless, joyful boy but a grown-up man, thinking deeply about a grave subject. "This is serious", he said, "it may end badly for Sasha",' recollects Kashkadamova. An hour later she was to face Maria Alexandrovna who 'pale and grave' ran through the letter, and asked Kashkadamova to look after the children in her absence: she was leaving immediately for St. Petersburg. Volodya booked for his mother a seat on the coach to Syzran; it was in vain that he knocked on the doors of friends and neighbours to beg someone to accompany her on the journey. No one volunteered to travel with the regicide's mother even as far as the railway station; and so His Excellency's widow left Simbirsk alone to fight for the life of her firstborn.

In St. Petersburg she spent nearly a month in the corridors of police headquarters and in the ante-chambers of the Public Prosecutor begging to be allowed to see her imprisoned children. On 30 March she saw Sasha for the first time. 'He wept, embraced her knees, and imploring her to forgive him the grief he had caused her, said: "Apart from the duty towards one's family, one has a duty towards one's country",' adding that every honest man must fight against the lawlessness and tyranny that oppress the nation. When she objected to the 'dreadful means' to which the conspirators had resorted, he replied: 'But what could one do when there were no other means?' He tried to prepare her for the worst and talked about the consolation she would find in the happier fate of the other children. She still tried to save him and knocked on all the doors of authority. Just before the trial she returned to Simbirsk for a day or two and told Kashkadamova that she expected a sentence of lifelong *katorga* (penal servitude); she planned to move to Siberia to be as near Alexander as possible. She would take her younger children with her, she said, and the older ones will manage on their own. Just about a year had passed since she wrote to His Excellency the Trustee of the Kazan Educational District, the confidential Counsellor P. N. Maslennikov: 'I hope that, with God's help, he [Alexander] will in future become a support for me and his younger brothers and sisters. . . .' Now she was ready to sacrifice herself for him and it seemed 'that she loved her older son more than all the other children'.

Alexander went on relentlessly to meet his destiny. Fearing that none of his comrades might be equal to the task of proclaiming their principles from the dock, he took this upon himself; he faced the judges as the leader of the conspiracy; the court, and the defendants, accepted him as such. The proceedings opened on 15 April 1887, three days after his twenty-first birthday, and lasted until 19 April. The trial was held *in camera*; only the closest relatives of the defendants were admitted. One of the survivors of the group, the graduate in Divinity, was to recollect that in the dock Alexander was just as calm as he used to be at students' meetings: 'He had taken his last and irrevocable decision.' To Lukashevich, whose nerves were shaky, he managed to whisper: 'You may talk against me if this will help you.' According to another survivor, 'the whole attention of those present and of the court was concentrated on Ulyanov'. ' "Why," he was asked, "did you not try to escape abroad?" "I did not want to escape—I would rather die for my country," he replied.' Even the Prosecutor paid a grudging tribute to his heroism and devotion to the cause: 'Ulyanov takes upon himself many deeds of which he is in fact not guilty.' His mother attended one session of the court and said later: 'I was surprised to hear how well Sasha spoke: so convincingly, so eloquently. I did not think that he could speak like that. But my grief was so maddening that I could not listen to him too long—I had to leave.'

In his statement of principles which he made on 18 April he spoke of the vague feeling of dissatisfaction which was gradually mounting in him since his early youth; but 'only the study of social and economic affairs gave [him] the deep conviction that the existing order of things was not normal; and then [his] vague dreams about freedom, equality, and brotherhood assumed strictly scientific, that is, socialist forms'. 'I understood that it was not only possible but necessary to change the social order.' Echoing Marx and Plekhanov, he said: 'Every country develops spontaneously, according to definite laws, goes through strictly determined phases and inevitably achieves social [i.e. socialistic] organization. This is the inevitable result of the existing order and of those contradictions which are inherent in it.' He posed the question of the individual's role in the transformation of society, saying that it was not in the power of one man to change the natural course of history—the individual could only put his intellectual resources at the service of an ideal and help to make society aware of its condition and its tasks. He then expressed his views which, on the face of it, should have prevented him from participating in the conspiracy: as any change in the social order can result only from a change in the consciousness of the society, there existed only one 'correct method' to bring about that change and that was propaganda of ideas by means of the printed word. 'But as all theoretical reflection led me to this conclusion, life was proving with object lessons that under the existing conditions it was impossible to take that road. With the government's attitude towards intellectual life, it was impossible to propagate not only socialist but even general cultural ideas.' He found it extremely difficult to engage even in 'scientific analysis of the problems'. He went on to delve into the state of Russian society and its inability to assert itself against the autocratic state. He spoke of the special responsibility of the educated people who represented the nation's consciousness and conscience, who alone had it in themselves to challenge the powers that be and advance the ideas that led to the transformation of society. But

our intelligentsia is so weak physically and so unorganized that at the present time they cannot enter into any open struggle; only in a terroristic form can they defend their right to think and to participate in social life. Terror is that form of struggle which has been created by the nineteenth century, the only form of self-defence to which a minority, strong only through its spiritual force and the awareness of its righteousness, can resort against the majority's awareness of physical force.

Again and again he underlined that the use of terror was not a matter of premeditation and free choice, but a bitter necessity: 'Of course, terror is not the intelligentsia's weapon in organized struggle. It is only a road which particular individuals take spontaneously when their discontent reaches extremity. Thus viewed, terrorism is an expression of the popular struggle and will last as long as the nation's needs are not satisfied. . . .' In Russia, went on Alexander, we have the possibility of developing our intellectual resources, but we are not allowed to use them in the service of our country.

The reaction acts oppressively against the majority; but the government, depriving the minority . . . of every chance to act in a legitimate manner, pushes it on the only road which is left . . . and all this affects not only reason but emotions as well. You will always find in the Russian nation a dozen people who are so devoted to their ideals and who feel so deeply their country's misfortune, that for them to die for their cause means no sacrifice. Such people cannot be intimidated. . . . I have succeeded in showing that terrorism is the natural product of the existing order—if this is so, then terrorism will continue. . . .

The official report of the trial was published only after 1917. Yet, in spite of the secrecy of the proceedings, the people at the time knew a great deal about its course, and Alexander's statement, his arguments, and the manner in which he expounded them spread widely by word of mouth. His stand in the dock was so evocative of the heroism of the 1881 martyrs that Alexander himself was indeed compared to Zhelyabov. The conspiracy was usually referred to as 'the case of Alexander Ulyanov and comrades'.[1] The death sentence was passed in the last week of April, but Maria Alexandrovna was still trying to get the sentence commuted; she went to her son's cell to beg him to ask for mercy. 'I cannot do that after all I

[1] This was by no means a later accretion on the Ulyanov legend lighting up Alexander in the reflected glory of the great Lenin. Indeed, it was Lenin in the first years of his political activity who was often referred to as 'Alexander Ulyanov's younger brother'.

have said in court. This would be false', was Sasha's answer. A young assistant prosecutor, Kniazev, was *ex officio* present at the meeting. He behaved with sympathetic discretion, standing aside. However, he did hear Alexander's reply, and, as if unable to overcome his admiration, exclaimed: 'He is right, he is right.' The death sentence could only be commuted to life-long incarceration in the Schlüsselburg fortress. 'Would you wish this for me, mother?' They both knew that this could be worse even than death. Maria Alexandrovna felt crushed and defeated. Sasha wanted to spend his last days reading. He was grateful to a friend who had sent him a newly published work on economics and finance, but he also wanted to have Heine's works in his cell. These, however, banned by censorship, were practically unobtainable. But here again, the same Kniazev, the young prosecutor, volunteered to supply them.

Maria Alexandrovna had not given up her struggle even now. St. Petersburg was full of rumours that the Tsar might be willing to spare the young lives of the conspirators, and these rumours were 'still nursing the unconquerable hope'. She rushed to the Peter-Paul fortress, where Sasha had been transferred. She talked to him through a double grille with a gendarme marching to and fro between mother and son. She wanted to convey to her son some of her feelings and she shouted: 'Take heart! Take courage!' These were to be her last words to him. On 8 May Alexander was hanged. She learned about the execution from a newspaper bought on the way to another prison—to visit Anna.

At Simbirsk Vladimir Ulyanov was graduating from the gymnasium. He had to obtain permission to sit his final examination, and on 18 April, the day of Alexander's great defiant speech in the St. Petersburg court, Vladimir wrote this brief application: 'To His Excellency Director of the Simbirsk classical gymnasium. Wishing to obtain matriculation, I have the honour humbly to ask His Excellency to admit me to examination. . . . Signed: Pupil of the Eighth Form, Vladimir Ulyanov.' He could not be at all sure that he would be admitted. He felt already the social ostracism to which the Ulyanovs were being subjected; he noticed how erstwhile friends of the family, even those who owed their education or career to his father, those who used to drop in almost daily for a chat or a game of chess, avoided them now, some studiously, some less so. And he wondered whether the Headmaster would not behave likewise. In truth, Fyodor Mikhailovich Kerensky was in trouble: the Ministry was censuring him for having encouraged and awarded a Gold Medal to a pupil who turned out to be a regicide—indeed, for having allowed his gymnasium to become a hotbed of subversion. There was no saying how such censure would affect the Headmaster's future career. A man of lesser character might have cleared his record in the eyes of authority and proven himself the Tsar's zealous subject by treating at least the regicide's brother with displeasure. That the Headmaster was deeply shocked and shamed by what the star of his school had done, there can be no doubt—Fyodor Mikhailovich was the Tsar's loyal subject. But he was also loyal to the memory of Ilya Nikolaevich and determined to stand by his family in their ordeal. So he not merely recommended that Vladimir should be allowed to sit for his examination; he also gave him this certificate of character:

Exceptionally talented, constantly diligent and accurate [Vladimir] Ulyanov was the first pupil in all forms; at matriculation he was awarded a Gold Medal as being the most deserving of it by his achievement, development, and behaviour. Neither within this gymnasium nor outside it has any single instance ever been noticed in which Ulyanov has either by word or by deed given ground for . . . disapproval.

Regardless of any risk to himself, the Headmaster behaved towards his favourite pupil with absolute fairness, and he was also anxious to free him from the fresh opprobrium. He spoke up as the friend of the Ulyanov family: 'Ulyanov's parents have always carefully watched over his education and moral development. . . . At the basis of [this] upbringing was religion and reasonable discipline. Good results of the domestic upbringing were evident in [Vladimir] Ulyanov's excellent conduct.' This was broadly true, even though the Headmaster's observations lagged behind the facts: he was evidently unaware of Vladimir's recent 'rejection' of religion, and he glossed over one or two minor incidents in which Vladimir's mockery did not spare even his teachers. However, the Headmaster added a cryptic remark: 'Watching more closely Ulyanov's private life and his character I could not fail to notice in him an excessive preference for seclusion and . . . a certain unsociability.'

He was certainly not trying here to insure himself against reproaches from above and to weaken the favourable opinion about his pupil: he was honestly and realistically describing Volodya's extreme inner reserve which prevented him from forming intimate friendships at school and kept him peculiarly distant even from close associates during his adult life. This was a character trait which Vladimir had in common with Alexander, and this thought might have given the good Headmaster a moment of uneasiness. But he hastened to reassure those for whom the certificate was intended, saying that 'Ulyanov's mother plans to be with her son all the time right through his studies at the University.' He thus implied that Alexander had gone astray only at St. Petersburg, where he was no longer under the beneficial influence of the parental home with its 'religion and reasonable discipline'. This was probably what the Ulyanovs' most charitable friends and what Maria Alexandrovna herself thought about the matter. She must have seen Kerensky during her brief stay in Simbirsk just before the trial and must have confided in him her plans to accompany Sasha to Siberia. Now she was indeed planning to move with her children to Kazan, for the authorities in St. Petersburg informed her that only in Kazan would Vladimir be allowed to seek entry to the University.

Vladimir wrote his first examination paper on Pushkin's *Boris Godunov* on 5 May, three days before his brother's execution. On the day Alexander went to the gallows, he sat over the mathematical papers. 'We were all terribly agitated', recollects a schoolmate, 'only Vladimir Ulyanov, seated behind his desk, wrote calmly and unhurriedly. . . .' 'We were given only six hours for doing our papers . . . Vladimir Ilyich finished and delivered his work earlier than the rest of us and was the first to leave the examination hall. . . .'

The newspapers reporting the execution had already reached Simbirsk when Volodya was doing his trigonometry and translating passages from Thucydides into Russian. During a week's interval before the oral examinations, his mother came home; her hair had turned white in the last few weeks. With her came Anna but only to leave at once for Kokushkino—she had been released on condition that she would stay under police supervision at her grandfather's rural estate. Vladimir's oral examination lasted from 22 May till 6 June. Meanwhile the house and its furniture was put on sale giving the town's gossips an excuse for coming in to gaze at the regicide's mother. Vladimir passed all tests *summa cum laude*; he was awarded his medal, but the School Council decided that it would not do to put the name 'Ulyanov' in the roll of honour on the marble plaque on which the names of all previous holders of the medal were engraved.

Vladimir's behaviour in these weeks shows his extraordinary self-control, but it also raises the question: just how strongly did the boy of seventeen, working so 'calmly and unhurriedly' on his examination papers, feel

64

about his brother and his family's tragedy? A fellow pupil of the school gives his reminiscences of a chance encounter with Volodya on the eve of one examination:

I shall never forget this warm May evening. . . . I went out . . . for a walk along The Crown . . . I was humming a song to myself. Passing by the summer house I noticed someone looking intently towards the distant horizon beyond the Volga. Paying no attention I walked by and sang quite loudly. 'Aren't you preparing for the exams?' I suddenly heard Volodya's voice. Happy to meet him, I approached him and noticed that he was peculiarly absorbed in something, and subdued. I sat next to him and began to admire the view of the Volga. Volodya remained silent and sometimes sighed deeply. 'What's the matter with you?' I asked at last. He turned his face towards me, wanted to say something but did not, and again withdrew within himself. I thought he was grieving over his father or worried about Alexander who, as we knew, had been arrested. . . . I tried to dispel his anguish . . . but it was no use. I knew that Volodya was sometimes gay, but that sometimes he was unsociable and in such moments avoided talking. . . . But the evening was so still, as if nature itself wanted to calm and reassure us. I said so to Volodya. After a moment of silence he told me that on 8 May Alexander had been put to death. I was stunned. Droopingly, slouchingly, Volodya sat next to me. Under the rush of thoughts it was impossible to speak. We sat so for a long time in silence. At last Volodya got up, and, saying nothing, we went towards the town. We walked slowly. I saw Volodya's deep grief but also had the feeling that just then a spirit of firm determination welled up in him. . . . Before parting I strongly grasped his hand. He looked into my eyes, responded to the handshake, and quickly turned and walked home.

From several other contemporary accounts we are given the same glimpse of the drooping, painstricken boy, struggling to contain his feelings within himself. This ability to control strong emotions was a family trait: we have seen it in Alexander. We find it also, more surprisingly, in his sister Olga. Though a year younger than

Volodya, she, too, sat for matriculation tests in these days; she, too, passed them brilliantly, and was also awarded the gold medal. 'She kept on coming to school . . . her self-control was amazing; she was as if turned into stone', says one of her school friends. She fainted, however, during a service to the memory of a head-mistress which took place on 9 May. 'Recovering, she said to me "Katya, yesterday he was executed." She said only this. . . .' And in her home, now put on auction, Maria Alexandrovna, dressed in black, but erect with dry eyes, was meeting the curious and the inquisitive with the icy question: 'Which piece of furniture do you wish to buy?'

In the next few months and years Vladimir was to think deeply about Alexander's fate, scrutinize his experience, and draw from it a moral for himself. It would be idle to speculate whether he would have ever decided to become a revolutionary if Alexander's martyrdom had not given a completely new direction to his life and thought. There never was in Tsarist Russia any lack of reasons which impelled young men from the intelligentsia to struggle against the existing social order; these reasons were decisive for Vladimir Ulyanov too. However, at the moment of Alexander's death he was still very far from the idea that he too might become a revolutionary. Up to 1 March 1887 he had been engrossed in the writings of great poets and novelists, in the masters of Greek and Latin prose, and, to some extent, in history. Politics or political economy had not even began to engage his attention. Contemporary social affairs were as remote to him as they could be to any a-political youngster. Leading a sheltered existence, successful at school, find-ing delight in the play of his expanding intellect and preparing for what everybody expected to be the great academic career of a classical scholar—hardly anything in his behaviour indicated that Vladimir Ulyanov might presently break out of this frame of mind and begin to search for roads to revolution. Only under the shock of Alexander's fate did the world of Volodya's childhood and adolescence collapse. Only then was his mind suddenly plunged into social and political issues and his own destiny began to take on an unexpected shape. The medium of intimate personal experience made articulate to Vladimir the general cause for revolution in Russia—as if the conditions of Russian society had refracted themselves through the family tragedy. And so, although one may assume that Vladimir Ulyanov would have become Lenin even if his brother had not died on the gallows, there can be no doubt about the impact of Alexander's martyrdom on his early development as a revolutionary. Lenin himself was aware of this and very briefly spoke about it to his wife and sisters; all the more significant is the circumstance that throughout his political career he never evoked in public, or even mentioned, his brother's life or death. The name of Alexander does not occur in any of Lenin's books, articles, speeches, or even in his letters to his mother and sisters. In all the fifty-five volumes of the latest and most complete Russian edition of his *Works*, Alexander is mentioned almost incidentally and only twice: in a purely factual statement in which Lenin answers a questionnaire (never completed or sent out); and in a letter in which Lenin, in 1921, recommended a certain Chebotarev: 'I have known Chebotarev', wrote Lenin, 'from the 1880s in connection with the case of [my] elder brother Alexander Ilyich Ulyanov hanged in 1887. Chebotarev is undoubtedly an honest man.' The omission of the 'my' in the sentence is characteristic. So extraordinary a reticence could not be ascribed to frigidity of feeling: on the contrary, it covered an emotion too deep to be uttered and too painful ever to be recollected in tranquillity.